PSYCHOLOGY AND THE SOUL

Otto Rank's

SEELENGLAUBE UND PSYCHOLOGIE

**Translated by
WILLIAM D. TURNER**

Martino Publishing
Mansfield Centre, CT
2011

Martino Publishing
P.O. Box 373,
Mansfield Centre, CT 06250 USA

ISBN 1-891396-61-7

Cover design by T. Matarazzo

Printed in the United States of America On 100% Acid-Free Paper

PSYCHOLOGY
AND THE SOUL

Otto Rank's

SEELENGLAUBE UND PSYCHOLOGIE

Translated by
WILLIAM D. TURNER

PHILADELPHIA
UNIVERSITY OF PENNSYLVANIA PRESS
1950

TRANSLATOR'S PREFACE

WHILE eighteen years have passed since Dr. Otto Rank published his *Seelenglaube und Psychologie,* the durability of his theses, and the shift in psychological thinking from German- to English-speaking peoples, have seemed to justify the present translation.

Because a psychological point of view is not a matter of sheer intellect, psychological convictions are apt to be firm, and psychological pioneers correspondingly rare. One really discovers a new point of view only through the painful relinquishment of an old one, and a translator as such can only prepare for this discovery to the extent of putting the new point of view into the learner's native language when it is not already there. If the present translation does just this much, and helps thereby to minimize the duplication of creative effort that already characterizes the helping professions, it will have served a genuine purpose. If also it can encourage some creativity beyond itself, it will not have failed its own philosophy.

Some professional readers who want only to ascertain what Rank has to say may wish that he had let his writings express simply the *result* of his movement away from Freud, rather than the movement as well. The severity of Rank's criticisms may make them more obnoxious; and the unsympathetic reader is not the only one whom Rank may anger, for neutral and sympathetic readers may have frequent cause for irritation with him. Two motives which underlay Rank's writing should not be disregarded. The first stemmed from the fact that his own developing point of view, and his criticism of the point of view he was rejecting, were sides of one coin. The second motive arose from Rank as a creative person whose overwhelming need to express himself left him with little or no readiness to consider his reader as a reader. We simply inherit the product of such motives, and claim or disclaim our heritage, as we ourselves may choose.

Thus, Rank's translated style and some of his theses will certainly be formidable enough at first to the lay reader who habitually reads quickly and only once. But then the person who is prepared to think and to feel about what he reads will discover that Rank's point of view is as new and as stimulating as it was two decades ago. A second difficulty with Rank will lie in his virtual obligation to use prose to transmit a thesis, much of which is inherently poetic and irrational. Life, experience, growth, the soul, and man's need to believe in his immortality can no more be contained within the sober lines of prose than within the bounds of logic. A reader's final and greatest struggle with Rank may well lie with his own will to deny his feelings about the meaning of what he reads and to deny that he is denying them. This experience is natural enough and quite beyond criticism, because any human being will have the same struggle. I comment upon it only to explain to some readers why so many others to whom they may refer this volume will finally lay it aside in more or less unrecognized anger and despair.

Psychology and the Soul reflects both elements of its title. Of the two, man's belief in his soul is so basic that it alone could have identified the book without misleading the reader. But the word "psychology" has also been retained because psychologies of one kind or another have come to hold significance for so many persons, because they are so often grasped with the hope that they will provide what no psychology can give, and because in a way they manifest the efforts of psychologists to save their own and others' souls. Perhaps Rank's central thesis is that intellectual psychology cannot give man the immortal soul he wants, but tends to destroy with doubt the soul which he does have.

I have had the usual difficulty in translating the German noun *Seele* into English. To a German-speaking person *Seele* means what an English word would mean to an English-speaking person if it could combine at one time some of the meanings of the English words "mind" and "soul." Our own ideology can help us here by reminding us of our tendency to think of the soul as being definitely allied with consciousness or the mind. In fact, we find it distasteful to think of our souls as though they had no connection with our minds. Eastern peoples, who can yearn for a Nirvana in which their identities are lost and their souls are fused with a cosmic soul, are almost incomprehensible to us who want to be "awake" during our particular variety of eternal life. While Rank reminds us that this conjunction of mind and soul has not always existed, I have nearly always translated *Seele* into "soul" with the reasonable hope that its *mental* connotation will be clear from the context when that is necessary.

The corresponding German adjective *seelisch* gives the greater difficulty. In the absence of an English adjective like "soully" I have used the word "spiritual," which may often confuse the reader unless he remembers that it connotes something that has to do with the living, conscious mind or self, and with the whole person who, as a human, must also live in a world of ideologies that are more real to him than he sometimes likes to admit. If the reader persists in reading this word with only its dualistic or ecclesiastical meaning in mind, he will generally miss Rank's point. He will follow the argument better if he remembers the intangible beliefs and values by which he inescapably lives, and if he remembers himself as a person who lives and wants to live eternally by them. Too many psychologies have offered consolation to their followers and creators by attempting to rationalize such spiritual matters out of existence. That this effort must be fruitless and that man must somehow face and cope with its futility are two of Rank's major assertions.

Where the German text and footnotes have cited non-English titles of references, I have given English titles which are followed in parenthesis by the titles as originally given. While this procedure is unusual in the translation of such works as the present one, I have felt that some English readers who may not read an original treatise in a foreign language will be gratified in being able at least to tell what a cited reference generally concerns.

In respect to both persons, Dr. Rank's dedication of *Seelenglaube und Psychologie* to Mrs. Beata Rank has been reproduced as he wrote it. I am indebted to Mrs. Helene Veltfort and Mme Estelle B. Simon for their permission to publish the present translation. Further, to the degree that this translation may have merit it really must be regarded as the result of several persons' efforts. The first of these is Dr. Rank himself, whose fertile approach to psychological matters was an irresistible incentive to me to translate him. A second person is Dr. Jessie Taft, whose genuine understanding of Rank I emulate. The third is Pearl Turner, whose intuitive grasp of Rankian concerns has made her my most stimulating colleague. And the fourth is Grace Good, whose typing of the manuscript left me free finally to escape from the words and to discover the story.

WILLIAM D. TURNER

School of Social Work
University of Pennsylvania
Philadelphia

CONTENTS

UNDERSTANDING
ONESELF AND OTHERS

> Religions die when one points out
> their truth. Science is the history of
> dead religions.   OSCAR WILDE

ALTHOUGH IT IS CUSTOMARY TO
say that scientific psychology originated with Aristotle who
first interpreted dreams psychologically, a thorough history
of psychology should cover all aspects of man's mental life
from its beginning. Prescientific and nonscientific psychology
has always been the true psychological discipline and the
source of all psychologies, including those that study the
soul scientifically. Scientific psychology which seems to know
very little about the soul claims to seek the truth about it,
but rejects the contributions of ancient beliefs, religion, and
myths to its interpretation. It performs experiments which
seem always to prove that the soul does not exist, and it lets
the more tolerant science of ethnology perform what constructive research it can. Psychoanalysis claims this neglected
area of psychology as its own, but it brings in its materialistic
psychology to "explain" the soul, instead of first trying to
relate its mental concepts to the spiritual sources which
generated them. Our present task, therefore, is not to apply
psychoanalysis or any other modern psychology to this problem, but to investigate the principles which govern the soul

1

concept as the source and object of psychological study. Our approach necessarily will be genetic and not historical.

This orientation brings us to the fundamental question of all psychology as science, which asks whether mental discipline is a proper concern for natural science or for philosophy, whether it is physics or metaphysics in the Aristotelian sense, and whether it is objective or subjective as natural science uses these terms. All psychological controversies, from Aristotle's scientific psychology to the conflicts between the various psychoanalytic schools, reduce to this question of a point of view. But in order to understand the controversies we must try to clarify the basic problem. Various stages of psychological knowledge disclose that the question of objective or subjective attitude and interpretation involves much more than two different kinds of observation. It concerns a dualism inherent in psychology itself, which I recognized when I once called psychology a relational science. This dualism involves the difference between psychology as self-knowledge and as a way of knowing others, or between psychology as a doctrine of self-awareness and as a "technique" for understanding and controlling others, whether the latter comprises a general science of character, reformative education, or therapy. The essential distinction is one between purely subjective psychology and applied objective psychology.

We shall see later how adequate such labels really are. One might assert that psychology's orientation is objective even though its original methods and values may possibly have been subjective. But I prefer to call it applied because it is used to influence others, and I shall liken it to primitive magic because it was founded on just as definite spiritual premises.

2

Although Aristotle's first attempt to release psychology from its spiritual bonds with the ego and to make a natural science out of it actually came quite late in man's development, his was an isolated effort, for psychology did not become an independent science until the nineteenth century. Then, logically enough, it began as a purely psychological science of consciousness in the Cartesian sense, and as a sensory psychology, psychophysics, or "psychology without a soul." As before, it left the soul to the philosophers, so that material for a history of modern mental discipline can be found only in psychological developments from the time of Descartes. Such material would also show that the soul gradually underwent transformation into the unconscious, while the doctrine of conscious phenomena remained a purely psychological discipline.

As a synthesis of the conscious and unconscious, Freud's psychoanalysis has both its strong and weak points. Freud wanted to carry a realistic psychology of self-awareness beyond consciousness, and to transform the mystical unconscious into an object of self-observation and objective investigation. He did succeed in expanding both psychology and the domain of consciousness, but since he explained the unconscious as realistically as sensory psychology had explained conscious phenomena, he excluded all its purely spiritual content. To be sure, he recognized spiritual content when he recognized the unconscious, but in explaining the unconscious materialistically he rejected the soul, because consciousness obviously involves something more than data about the outer world. He tried to explain the added elements by referring to the unconscious, while conceiving of the unconscious itself as a sediment of reality. Yet the unconscious contains more than past reality, since part of it

3

is as unreal or supernatural as the soul has always been. Originally, the soul was a purely inner, spiritual, and supernatural entity which became a matter of externals only at the hands of scientific psychology.

Although psychology may be a natural science, its spiritual basis defies explanation in terms of natural science or of psychology, because the psyche is neither a mere function of the brain nor a sublimation of instinct. Scientific psychology has tried to explain both impulse-man and brain-man on a common psychological basis, but as Bleuler frankly confesses, this attempt has left "a large hiatus."[1] The brain is just an instrument on which mental processes are played, and sexual impulse only one of their many expressions. Even if it were possible to comprehend all mental phenomena scientifically, the most important part of psychology, which concerns self-awareness, would remain unexplained because it is utterly subjective.

Although the value of this self-awareness lies in its subjectivity, the psychology concerned with it actually fails to disclose *one's own* mental life to oneself in the way that introspection is supposed to do. Introspection seems to be one of man's more recent and unnatural acquisitions, unsuited to the attainment of subjective self-awareness. It is more natural for man to project his own mental life on others than to learn about it directly through introspection. Projection has never been explained, probably because it is man's most characteristic and pervasive mental act. We shall come to understand it better; for the moment I should like to suggest how it operates in scientific psychology.

[1] Bleuler, *Natural History of the Soul and of Its Conscious Interpretation* [Naturgeschichte der Seele und ihres Bewusstwerdens] (Berlin: 1921), p. 54 ff.

As is well known, scientific psychology soon began to study thought processes. But the "method of association" which the young science had at its disposal had to characterize the thought of a person other than the experimenter. Although the results yielded by this method were said to have general significance, the experimenter himself was implicitly excluded from them as far as the experimental setting and outcome were concerned. Even psychoanalysis, which had laid aside the "objective" associative method for that of "free" association, betrays this same unpsychological character. For if an analyst's real aim is to discover general laws of the mental life of his patient, he at least should be included in the method no matter what the theoretical consequences. In practice, the analyst actually feels excluded from his method the more he tries to urge his psychology on the other person; so that for the same reason I called psychology relational in my *Genetic Psychology* (Genetische Psychologie, Vol. II, p. 13), one may characterize the practical psychology of understanding man scientifically as a *projective* discipline.

Just as we are apt to speak about *other* persons when questions of morality or education arise, what we really want at all times is to practice psychology *of* others as well as *on* them. And while it is understandable that we may require or possibly allow others to alter their own behavior, psychology still claims to be a discipline primarily concerned with knowledge of self, and tries paradoxically to win such knowledge from others and to test it out on them. In trying to defend its objective method, scientific psychology asserts that the object of its observation and research cannot also be its subject. But this logical difficulty is not as important as the emotional resistance that underlies it, for everyday experience proves that one's own ego can be even a fairly constant object of self-observation, and that the same errors inherent in such observation appear in studies of one's own projected psychology in others, be they students, patients, friends, or loved ones. Although natural science ideology easily inclines one to neglect differences which perhaps are more important in psychology than elsewhere, one does not need to get involved with the individual personality factors which are so difficult to establish, in order to sense the difference between the thought processes of a skilled experimenter and those of the average person upon whom he experiments. Nor does one need such involvement in order to recognize that inferences from one person to another are not automatic, or that the psychologist who is really excluded from his findings on others has some right to assume one psychology about psychologists and another about those whom they psychologize.

It seems to me that *the psychologist may be really involved in his findings only to the degree that he succeeds in projecting his psychology on others.* To be sure, he is usually unaware of this projection because he believes that he infers from the psychology of the person he studies to others and, therefore, to himself. Although one could well say that the results should be almost the same under these two conditions, it is the psychological attitude behind them which is important. For it seems to me that what we are really dealing with is an emotional basis for not wanting to use one's own ego as an object of psychological study. None of us really want to observe or know ourselves. Such observation is not natural to us, and it hurts and hinders far more than it helps us. Why else should we claim so often that we need to know ourselves better in order to make our self-consciousness more bearable?

6

The objective psychology which began as magic became the pedagogue's, the social worker's, and the therapist's means of understanding, influencing, and controlling other persons. The subjective side of psychology is actually not a practical source of self-knowledge, because it tends to disturb our spontaneous action which is projective. The original naïve tendency to project is anti-introspective, and objective scientific psychology is always projective and therefore subjective even when it looks like a psychology of the other person. Psychology's adjustment to this inevitable fact has been so rational that it actually postulates knowledge of self as a prerequisite to knowing others. But knowledge of self is not necessary to the understanding of others, because this understanding can be achieved intuitively or even objectively the less the knower tries to understand himself through his observation of others. I do not believe that psychology began as self-observation or introspection with self-knowledge as its goal. Of course, it has always been a subjective discipline, but its particular brand of subjectivity has exhausted itself in a form of self-portrayal which is as different from self-awareness as it can possibly be. Scientific psychology certainly must have arisen objectively as a discipline for influencing and controlling others. Self-knowledge was only its by-product which it first tolerated and then welcomed.

It seems to me that this self-knowledge is responsible for the modern type of psychologist who in turn seeks it for himself and others. Expressed somewhat ironically, it is as though man had to find some use for his apparently worthless self-awareness, and so created out of it a science oriented not to the practical understanding of others but to a "scientific" justification of his pedagogical and therapeutic techniques. It turns out, then, that objective psychology owes

7

its exalted value just to its subjective relation to our personal ego, and that the objective portion of our observation of others is unscientific because it is practical. The impracticality of a psychology restricted to self-observation is shown by our inability to imagine how such a scientist could qualify as a pedagogue, psychiatrist, or applied psychologist. Unless one can *use* his introspective skill he can only meditate upon his own thoughts and feelings, and can only become what the practical psychologist often calls a "compulsive neurotic" or, at best, a philosophical thinker. Most of us feel that self-knowledge is worth the effort only when we can *use* it to understand, control, or "help" others—as we so often rationalize our intent to control.

Psychoanalysis itself is a lively subject for psychological research, for it combines the objective and the subjective, the technical and the purely theoretical, the natural scientific and the social scientific aspects of psychology in a way never before achieved. However, this seems to make psychoanalysis the final chapter and not just a new trend in the history of psychology. For in psychoanalysis, as in the violent controversies over its significance and province, we encounter the old fundamental problem of whether it is physics or metaphysics, medical or philosophical, or psychological or spiritual. Now it is obviously all of these, as every real psychology always was, is, and presumably will be. Just the peculiar combination of such contradictory elements composes this doctrine of psychoanalysis which began as a technique for influencing others and ended as a new metaphysics of the soul, and embodied in its own unsolved problems those of all psychology.

The affective power of psychoanalysis lies just in its scientific weakness of being both psychology and spiritual

8

doctrine, and of failing to differentiate at all between these two aspects. Were psychoanalysis more definitely the one or the other, it could not be the unique fusion that it is. In the terminology of our natural science era, it combines the causal way of thinking which seeks to explain facts by reducing them to relationships expressed as natural laws, with the cultural way of thinking which tries to comprehend the meaning and structure of mental phenomena. Yet in this dual role psychoanalysis has limits that are manifested most clearly in the exaggerated systems of Adler and Jung, each of whom emphasizes one side of dualistic psychology at the expense of the other. The hypercausality of Jung's phylogenetic theory led him to reduce the principle of psychological causation to an absurdity, while the hyperfinality in Adler's individual psychology kept him from seeing anything but structural tendencies. Paradoxically, Jung was opposed to the natural scientific elements of his system which he overextended in his phylogenetic causality; and Adler disregarded the actual cultural scientific foundation of his own individual psychological view. Psychoanalysis itself, which would like to do justice to both problems, neglects reality and values the psychic, which it then tries to explain on the basis of reality.

Yet only psychoanalysis so clearly betrays the inherent unity of these two sides of psychology. Originally its ideas were purely therapeutic, and they tended to release the psychological type of person from his compulsion to understand others in order to learn about himself. This growth in understanding through others helped the knower therapeutically, because it signified love and justified his own personality. But it was just this unpsychological aspect of affectionate understanding that brought the good therapeu-

9

tic view of psychoanalysis to grief, for it was finally the understanding psychoanalyst who sent the self-conscious neurotic back to the very self-knowledge from which he wanted to escape. On the whole, psychoanalysis failed therapeutically because it aggravated man's psychologizing rather than healed him of his introspection. The theory which had evolved from a therapeutically oriented understanding of man into a scientifically motivated knowledge of self yielded only a psychology of the psychological type of man who still yearned to become unpsychological and more like the "normal man" whose psychology science always wanted to find but could not, because he had none.

Thus psychology, as a science and as a scientific technique for influencing others, is basically an interpretation of another's mental life in terms of one's own attitudes of feeling and willing. When we cannot change or get rid of another person, we can at least interpret him in terms of ourselves. And yet our individual psychology also reflects others and their reaction to our projection of our psychology upon them. In short, we not only express hostility toward others and try to control them by interpreting them as *we will*, but we reinterpret ourselves in their image, and call the process love. In this sense psychology is a reciprocal reflex phenomenon, or a kind of *Fata Morgana* of our real selves, which we see only in the mental mirroring of ourselves in others, and of them in us.

This brings us back to the problem of the real object of psychology. At first this object was the supernatural and non-human soul, but with the gradual disappearance of ancient spiritual belief from his consciousness, *man* himself became the object of psychological interest and research. In this sense religion is just as good a psychology as our

10

scientific psychology is a doctrine of the soul which it denies. The current interest in psychology is essentially a pursuit of religion and of a belief in the soul. The difference between religion and psychology lies in the fact that religion is a belief in the soul, while scientific psychology denies the soul as it pursues the spiritual belief inherent in its own interest in the individual ego. In other words, from religion to modern psychology, human evolution is nothing but a progressive individualization of spiritual belief which gradually turned from the universal soul to the individual soul or ego. Non-scientific psychology does not understand the soul but wants to postulate it, and modern psychology, which wants to pass judgment on it, concedes the *possibility* of its existence and postulates it as an object of research without really admitting that it exists.

There is a third and pre-final stage in the evolution of psychology, in which psychology and not man or his soul, becomes the object of psychological study. This is quite proper, for psychology itself has gradually abandoned its original denial and negation of the soul, and has offered substitute objects not only for man's lost belief in the soul but for man who lost that belief. Just as religion represents a psychological commentary on the social evolution of man, various psychologies represent our current attitudes toward spiritual belief. In the animistic era, psychologizing was a *creating* of the soul; in the religious era, it was a *representing* of the soul to one's self; in our era of natural science it is a *knowing* of the individual soul.

Yet we still cling to the original spiritual belief, which was a naïve belief in immortality. Only unlike animistic man we do not do this consciously; we are ashamed of it and we deny it. What persists as unconscious spirituality in us all is

11

not the biological animal of psychoanalytic theory, but the mental spirit which can never be contained by a materialistic terminology. Our psychological heritage from the race is the soul, the spiritual belief, the ancient psychology in which we all unconsciously believe, but which our modern psychology helps us consciously to deny.

This view conforms to the increasingly recognized fact that primitive man was less realistically oriented than is modern man. He was unrealistic, spiritual, and more concerned with the supernatural powers he projected into nature than with the causes that might explain it. To the extent that we have become more realistic, we have to preserve within ourselves the spiritual forces that no longer find any place in our outer world. Primitive man recognized the soul consciously, believed in it, and filled his world with this spiritual belief so that it became as unreal as himself. We are psychologists, so oriented psychologically by our denial of spirituality that we "motivate causally" what is really motivated spiritually, and try to substitute for belief a knowledge which ultimately rests on belief in the soul. This brings all the contradictions and irrational elements into our mental lives and psychological systems. Primitive man projected the soul into his total reality and universe, and arrived at a supernatural, primitively magical, and ultimately religious point of view. In accepting both reality and ourselves as being realistic, we no longer project so much onto the other world as onto other men. Our projection onto the other person, and its reaction upon ourselves, comprise objective psychology.

RELIGION AND BELIEF
IN THE SOUL

> *God has made the soul so like him-*
> *self that there is in heaven and on*
> *earth nothing quite so like God as*
> *the human soul.*
>
> MEISTER ECKEHART

IN 1914 I MADE A STUDY OF THE psychoanalytic attempt to understand primitive spiritual belief in relation to the psychoanalytic view of primitive peoples. Starting from literary examples of the Double motif,[1] I conceived of primitive belief in a body-soul as an expression of man's deeply rooted belief in immortality. The body-soul was originally thought of as a second, purely material self like the physical self which it survived, and the fact that primitive man first localized it in his shadow or mirror-image suggests that the loss of his own individuality seemed to him almost more inconceivable than unbearable. At the earliest stage of his so-called spiritual belief in the soul, man seemed to deny rather than fear his own death, for his idea of an immortal body-soul comprised a denial of death which canceled all possible threats to his perpetuity.

[1] "The Double" (Der Doppelgänger), *Imago*, Vol. III, 1914. Published separately in the Internationaler Psychoanalytischen Verlag, 1925.

13

Thus the facts of death and of the individual's denial of death brought the idea of the soul into being; and, at a time when life was beginning to acquire a spiritual character, the problems of death and of its denial through belief were imbedded in an immortal body-soul which simulated and survived the ego as its Double. The problem of death seemed to face primitive man less in the form of anxiety, which he could deny, than in the death of others, which at first he did not have to ascribe to himself. When he finally did refer this experience of others to himself he took his first step toward an intuitive psychology of understanding others. Such a psychology is obviously contrary to its logical and scientific counterpart, which invites one to use one's own experience to understand others.

Perhaps it is the application of our subjective psychology of dreams to the spiritual life of primitive man which has led so many ethnologists of our time to assume that the dream roles of the dead induced primitive man to believe in a soul independent of his body. But dreams were real to primitive man, and they presented him with the souls of other persons both living and dead rather than with his own. Dreams even "delude"[2] us in the same way since they exhibit dead or absent persons far more often than our own selves. I regard primitive man's reference of such dreams to himself as a second, conflictive stage in the evolution of spiritual belief which followed an initial "narcissistic" stage; so that just as his shadow or mirror-image allowed him to believe in his own body-soul, his realistic dreams induced him to accept the survival of the souls of others. Thus his

[2] As is well known, the German word "Traum" (dream) has the same stem, "dreug," as "trügen" or "tauschen" (to delude). In other languages the word for "dream" is related etymologically to that for "sleep."

14

tormenting dreams of a "spirit" of the dead compelled him to concede immortality to others, to his enemies, and particularly to victims of murder. The idea of his *own* soul, which materialized as a snake, a bird, or as his breath, which left the body to lead an independent and often creative life, seems more like a secondary referral of his dream of another person's soul to himself. For the dream presents itself to one's ego in an objective and not a subjective form, and it is more a spiritual phenomenon than a psychological problem.[2a]

I cannot even begin to suggest what superstitions, religious ideas, and psychological views sprang from the original acceptance of others' immortality and from the consequences of such acceptance. This concession more than anything else produced the psychological problem of anxiety which man's belief in his own immortality had so far masked. This anxiety appeared first as a fear not of living persons but of the spirits of dead or slain persons, and of demons whose reappearance was ascribed to a thirst for revenge rather than to a love of life. Yet because the spirit of the murder victim could torment the murderer in his dream, his immortality was really more certain than that of persons who had died natural deaths. In a certain sense, then, violent death became a source of immortality, as later superstitions and the figures of Christ and Joan of Arc illustrate. Perhaps this idea also explains why primitive and ancient cults conferred the "sacrifice" as an honor only upon certain individuals, and also why a murderer always took the trouble to destroy his victim by devouring, dismembering, or burning him, with the obvious intent of robbing him of his greater chance for immortality which his role as victim had given him.

[2a] Concerning the whole theme of the dream, see the chapter "Dream and Reality" below.

In any event, the whole complex of ideas of a final and an immortalizing death led to the primal tabu against murder. The source of this prohibition was not external but lay within the individual himself, for tabu did not emerge from a growing consciousness of law, but from an inner threat to the self and its immortality. A dead person found no release until he had come after his murderer, killed him, and robbed him of his collective immortality, It is obvious, then, that our current legal consciousness, which is maintained by legalized prohibitions and regulations, sprang originally from an inner spiritual threat rather than from an external psychological one. This is indicated by the primitive belief which "causally" explained a murderer's natural death as the vengeance of a demon. Yet, like most causal explanations, this psychological one was based on spiritual belief. The *jus talionis,* or "eye for an eye," from which our criminal law has grown, probably rested on the animistic premise that the murderer had to die anyway since his act had invited a demon's vengeance. In killing the other person the murderer always killed his immortal soul, which even a belief in a Double had fully protected. Thus all tabus, persisting as custom, morals, or law, came to preserve man's immortality rather than his life, so that primitive man attempted to reconcile evil spirits in order to preserve this immortality.

The first "legal" or mutual pact not to kill is found in totemism which, in contrast to criminal law, guaranteed immortality and not life alone. Totemism also offered the first compromise between an enhanced awareness of the real meaning of death and a tenacious belief in immortality. In order to prove this latter point we must consider the other, creative side of immortality belief, which made up the real content of totemistic systems.

At its inception, totemism was a primitive belief in the soul.[3] The spirits of one's ancestors were then sacred and tabu not only because they were to be feared, but because immortality belief gave them the power to perpetuate mankind, and hence the individual. According to primitive Australian belief, the animal, plant, or stone totem entered and impregnated woman, and underwent rebirth in the process of animating the embryo.[4] The physical father had nothing to do with this process, for only the spirit of the dead could give the child a soul, and the living person needed his soul for himself. This principle, rather than any realistic motive, accounts for the totemistic marital restrictions which are found both in the strict exogamous regulations of primitive man and in surviving marital customs which leave the impregnation of a bride to the functioning deity. The basic idea that the father can beget but not animate also appeared in defloration ceremonies practiced by priests of ancient cults and in the attendant *jus primae noctis,* or "right of the first night." In the sexual abstinence practiced during the so-called "Tobias night"[5] a husband wanted to insure his soul and his immortality, because such abstinence made it pos-

---

[3] J. Winthuis stresses this point, particularly in *Hermaphroditism among Central Australian and Other Peoples. An Attempt to Solve the Central Problem of Ethnology on the Basis of Primitive Thought.* (Das Zweigeschlechterwesen bei den Zentralaustraliern und andern Völker. Lösungsversuch der ethnologischen Hauptprobleme auf Grund primitiven Denkens), Leipzig, 1918.

[4] See my *Socio-psychological Parallels to Children's Theories of Sexuality.* (Völkerpsychologische Parallelen zur den infantilen Sexualtheorien.) The incompleteness of these parallels, as far as the difference between child and primitive is concerned, is considered elsewhere.

[5] According to the Book of Tobit, the husband normally dies during the bridal night because, instead of abstaining so as to save his soul, he loses it in the act of reproduction. This is also the esoteric meaning of the virginity tabu.

17

sible for the dead to give up their homeless, unused souls, and it enabled the living husband ultimately to obtain sexual gratification without being responsible for conception. Animation of the unborn child by the dead or their spirits was an esoteric attempt to reconcile these spirits because the husband imposed sexual abstinence on himself not only to let them animate the child but also to convert the menace of their inevitable return into a guarantee of his own existence and perpetuation. Instead of letting them return with evil purpose, he made their return a benevolent one and kept his own soul from entering the new human being.

Hence the first sexual restrictions encountered in primitive exogamy and in all subsequent marital restraints of civilized peoples were not the results of external authority and regulation, but as shown earlier in relation to law, they were voluntary, spontaneous, and individual acts of self-protection. In animating the embryo, the dead person proved as serviceable as the living one, who was then left free to preserve his own soul. With the exception of psychoanalysts, who regard aversion to incest as a defense against an unconscious incest-wish, those authorities who explain exogamy in terms of such an aversion fail to account for incest itself. Psychoanalysis only raises the new problem of the incest-wish which seems to be less pronounced in primitive man than psychoanalysis finds in modern children,[6] who often enough view their whole world through the eyes of their elders. The primitive idea of incest was different from, and broader than, that implicit in our current legal and social family structure. The tribe or clan was divided into two or more groups whose male and female constituents were com-

---

[6] See my book: *The Incest Motif in Poetry and Saga* (Das Inzest-Motiv in Dichtung und Sage). Second, enlarged edition, 1926, especially with reference to group marriage, 408 ff.

18

pletely related by blood because they belonged to the same totem or spiritual reservoir. Although Winthuis ingeniously envisioned the totem as bisexual, it seems rather to have been asexual or non-sexual in character, because it was not responsible for procreation or birth, but only for spiritual animation. Prohibition of marriage within such a group appears to have had the esoteric significance both of guaranteeing fecundation of the wife by the spirits of the dead, which gradually became united into a single generic totem, and of excluding or exempting males from the process of fecundation. The man who was obliged to take a wife from a clan of a different totem received some guarantee that she would not be endangered or impregnated by intercourse with her "foreign" husband, and that he could experience sexual relations with her without running the risk of losing his own soul during the animation of the embryo. In effect, he was saved from the threat of having to assume the animating role of the totem, which would rob him of his soul and his immortality. The related concepts of incest and exogamy show again how external prohibitions which end in custom and law originated as purely inner, spontaneous, voluntary actions which were related not to real facts but to spiritual relationships.

Moreover, our view would explain another, yet unsolved puzzle of group psychology. Even today one frequently refers to the ignorance of certain primitive groups regarding the relationship between sexual intercourse and conception[7]

---

[7] Fr. Reitzenstein: "The Causal Connection between Sexual Intercourse and Conception, in the Beliefs and Customs of Primitives and Civilized Peoples." (Der Kausalzusammenhang zwischen Geschlechtsverkehr und Empfängnis in Glaube und Brauch der Natur und Kulturvölker) *Zeitschr. f. Ethnologie*, 1909, vol. 41, pp. 644-83. See also Malinowski's recent observations on the Trobriand Islanders, among whom so-called matriarchy exists (see below).

without being able to explain correctly how such realistically oriented primitives could have gone so long without having observed such a fundamental fact. Although it may seem plausible that the long interval between intercourse and conception, and primitive man's inadequate powers of observation could have delayed recognition of this fact, we still have a problem which is soluble in relation to its esoteric foundations alone and not to reality. There was a motive for denying the existence of this relation even after it was noticed. If the foregoing explanation of totemistic systems is correct, it becomes no great task to explain primitive man's unusual attitude toward this relationship, for by denying the implications of his increasing knowledge and insight into the relation between intercourse and conception, primitive man could preserve his original spiritual belief which totemism manifested as a closed system. If it were primitive man himself who gave life to the child, the whole structure of his spiritual belief and of his religious and social systems which rested on it would go to pieces, and this would be particularly true of spiritual belief whose perpetuation primitive man had insured in totemism, in which he allowed the dead to animate the child in order to preserve his own soul. Hence denial and not ignorance of the relationship between intercourse and conception was the basic premise of totemistic spiritual belief, just as denial and not ignorance supported belief in a primitive body-soul. The preservation of spiritual belief in totemism, which was to decline with increasing recognition of the nature of reproduction, was of vital importance to primitive man, and, as we shall see, not to him alone, for we shall encounter such things time and again in the unbelievably persistent attempts which man has made over the course of his development both to defend his belief in the immortality of his soul against the combined testimony of his senses, his reason, and his knowledge, and to preserve this belief in religious, social, and scientific institutions. As suggested before, the last of these possible attempts is psychology itself.

We should like to determine how far back in the history of man's spiritual life this point of view may be applied. It seems to me that matriarchy, which was totemism's immediate successor, was a further attempt on man's part to harmonize his progressively more meaningful sexual relationships with his belief in totemistic metempsychosis. The appearance of animals as agents of spiritual fecundation in totemism seems to indicate that primitive man was aware of natural sexual processes, or that, like our children, he at least believed they applied to animals.[8] Spirits used animals to exercise their impregnating function even under Christianity. Years ago I was able to use the materials of ancient myth to show that legends about heroic births[9] generally depicted animals as the protecting and nurturing mother, and rarely as the begetting father. It was actually not a simple matter of the totem animal reducing spiritual fecundation to completely realistic and naturalistic terms, for the totem animal did not provide a rational explanation of fertilization.

[8] Malinowski's contradictory report on the Trobriand Islanders (The Father in Primitive Psychology, 1927) evidences a somewhat too realistic attitude on the part of the observer. There is no reason to doubt that this is the belief of primitives, or that it precludes their having knowledge different from their belief. Even our own mental life juxtaposes unrelated and irreconcilable knowledge and beliefs.

[9] The Myth of the Birth of the Hero (Der Mythus von der Geburt des Helden), Vienna and Leipzig, F. Deuticke, 1908. Second, enlarged edition, 1922.

21

In many instances, of which the Heavenly Serpent is one example, it was rather a matter of a primal spirit animal, which was originally symbolized esoterically as bisexual, now appearing exoterically as a realistic representative of monosexuality.

There now seem to be a number of indications that at a certain stage this primal, spiritual connotation of animals was a purely maternal one like that evidenced later at a social level in matriarchy. The basic proof of this point, which I have already drawn from primitive thought, lies in the fact that animals which embodied the soul in totemistic systems appeared later on in a maternal role more appropriate to a mammal. To be sure, this was scarcely the first incarnation of the soul which employed small animals such as snakes, toads, mice, or even birds as overt symbols. The pre-totemistic belief of the Semang tribe (Malay Peninsula interior) and other groups used birds as primal spirit animals. At this stage the animal was killed in order that the spirit dwelling within it could be freed to fertilize the embryo (Winthuis, p. 175), while at a later stage the animal was not killed, because it was basically identified with man himself and represented his immortal part. At the sexual stage of man's development the esoteric meaning of birds as spirit animals was carried by an exoteric, phallic symbol, while more recent totem animals such as the Australian kangaroo were more maternal in form.

In contrast with the maternal significance of mammals, small animals symbolic of that which "creeps and flies" seem to have first symbolized the animating principle of spiritual (not paternal) reproduction which entered the mother so readily. In later superstitions these small animals represented the soul which escaped from the dreamer's mouth as he slept, and returned by the same path before he awakened. At first they were incarnations of the soul itself, then of the child as bearer of the soul,[10] and then of the phallus only after the father was recognized as the fertilizing agent. This development apparently followed a course typical for all such symbols, from an originally spiritual connotation of the soul, through a "bisexually" symbolic one, to one that was finally monosexual and realistic.

In order to understand the full meaning of these spirit and totem animals, we must consider woman's role in this animistic but scarcely primitive age. Up to this point we have said nothing of woman who stood apart from the wholly masculine evolution of primitive spiritual belief, just as though she had no soul. The fact that the child grows in the uterus and emerges from it did not disturb primitive irrealism. Even had primitive man been concerned only with observing and not with drawing conclusions from what he observed, it would scarcely have occurred to him to wonder how the embryo might have entered the mother in the first place, since, assuming his ignorance of natural processes of conception, there was no fact to imply that something had to enter a woman in order to explain the child's ultimate appearance. Indeed, the child could grow inside the mother just as a fruit or blossom grows on a tree. We find such an idea in every myth and legend, from the Garden of Eden to contemporary German superstition; Homer used it in his penetrating human simile; and it declined only in our allegory of the "family tree."[11] Is it the logical conclusion

---

[10] See my opinion regarding "small animals" in *The Trauma of Birth* (Das Trauma der Geburt), 1924, in which even the toad is dignified as uterine symbol.

[11] See the section on the family tree (Stammbaum), in Part I of my *Technique of Psychoanalysis* (Technik der Psychoanalyse), 1926.

from the child back to his invading precursor, or is it the dull memory of our own prenatal period, which we might still prove psychologically to be an instinctive longing to return to the womb?[12] Perhaps there is no need for such an assumption if we suppose instead that animistic man knew about reproductive processes but had to deny them in order to sustain his belief in immortality. In any event, the whole totemistic spiritual belief, which was created to preserve a purely narcissistic spiritual belief based on the Double, was now impossible unless man assumed that something entered the uterus in order to effect fertilization. We know from later myths and folklore that souls of the dead were thought to "dwell on" in certain places which we may certainly regard as uterine symbols. Still other legends show unequivocally that man returned to the place whence he came, which was obviously the womb. According to later belief, spirit-souls actually came from the place to which the souls of the dead had returned.[13] Even in totemistic spiritual doctrine we find the dead and their yet unborn souls associated with definite places which later superstition made so numerous that spirits could be found in every animal, spring, and tree.

The esoteric meaning of matriarchal institutions seems to me to lie in the fact that woman first appeared there as bearer of the soul, or as a noble vessel which sheltered the soul and passed it on to the child. Woman then represented the first *human* concretion of the soul or generic totem, who received the dead and animated her children with their spirit. An explanation for the importance of this humanized,

[12] See *The Trauma of Birth* (Das Trauma der Geburt), 1924.
[13] I have assembled the corresponding material in *The Myth of the Birth of the Hero* (Mythus von der Geburt des Helden), 1908, and in *The Lohengrin Saga* (Lohengrinsage), 1911.

24

totemistic role of woman seems to lie in matriarchal social structure and in its derived religious cults of the mother-god. For in the totemistic sense of identification of each individual with the totem, woman underwent gradual promotion from her role of soul-bearer to one of such identification. Thus, man's prohibition against killing the totem animal was his protection against the loss of his soul and his guarantee of immortality. For originally the totem animal was killed to obtain its soul for the new organism, as the pre-totemistic spirit-bird of the Semang people exemplified, so that the spirit bird became a bird of death which carried the soul to heaven. This role also appeared in the fable of the stork, whose nursery vulgarization apparently seeks to give a child this deeply rooted belief that souls come from the land of the dead.[14]

In matriarchal ideology woman herself became this spirit animal in whom the souls of the dead lay dormant until she gave them life again. By this time woman as wife and mother became as sacred as the totem or the soul had been, and immortal by virtue of her immunity to injury and death. While she had once been only its *medium,* she now came to represent the soul itself and to be identified with it. This is the meaning of the myth of Psyche, who was an overt representation of the soul from a feminine point of view. The idea of woman as representative of the soul not only affected subsequent folk tales about fairies, which women supposedly created, but also perhaps explains the ecclesiastical sacrament of the indissolubility of marriage, according to which husband and wife become one in spirit as well as flesh.

---

[14] See my volume *The Lohengrin Saga* (Lohengrinsage, 1911), and its underlying spiritual myth of the Knight and the Swan (Ritter mit dem Schwan), who came from the land of the spirits and returned to the land of the dead.

25

This new spiritual doctrine of the *mother,* who not only brings a child into the world but gives it its soul without losing her own, was expressed in the social divisions characteristic of matrilineal family law, under which the mother's brother supplanted the father, whose children then belonged to their mother. It seems to me that our narrow concept of incest, which implies only a prohibition of sexual relations with one's mother, first appeared in such a matrilineal system. This prohibition had an animistic basis which allowed the mother to become an invulnerable bearer of the soul, and a bulwark of the father's immortality rather than his chattel. Group marriage coeval with matriarchy held no offense against more than one brother marrying one and the same woman even though she were their blood sister, because as in totemism it was a matter of spiritual heritage rather than blood relationship.[15] Thus matriarchy, which was to be supplanted later by a family structure oriented around the father, was the third, humanized stage in the development of spiritual belief, which was precipitated by an expanding knowledge and recognition of natural life processes. Yet the basic problem of primitive man was not the future but the present, and not the riddle of birth but that of death. The naïve, narcissistic belief in a body-soul which perpetuated man's own bodily self beyond sleep and death, is obviously related to this latter problem. The second, totemistic stage could only support a belief in an immortal soul because it had to give up this naïve narcissism in order to assure man a form of soul transmigration like that of natural reproduction. The third, or matriarchal, stage finally accepted human

---

[15] As pacts with the Devil betray, blood was regarded as the seat of the soul only at a later stage. Apparently all these ideas, which later custom and law established so firmly, originated not from realistic demands but from spiritual motives which in many instances were opposed to reality.

sexual processes for what they were, because current spiritual belief was concretized in the wife or mother. Woman owed her original social esteem to her totemistic role of soul-bearer. But since primitive man allowed the spirit of his ancestor to enter the embryo in order to save his own soul, he traded a part of his belief in individual immortality for one in collective immortality. Just as death had created belief in an immortal soul, sexuality was used to preserve this spiritual belief from knowledge of natural life processes, because with its help one could achieve a realistic if not an individual immortality in one's descendants. In this fashion the original ego-psychology, or doctrine of the soul, became a collective sexual psychology which was only a renewed attempt to negate death with the help of the same biological reality that spiritual belief had previously denied.

Thus, totemism no longer involved an individual spirit of the dead, but a spirit embodied in a generic totem, which passed from the dead to the newborn child and, at the death of the latter, into the next generation. In contrast to the strict social regulation of sex characteristic of exogamy, primitive man created within his totemistic ideology a kind of nonmaterialistic promiscuity, because he comprehended all souls in a generic totem which animated all children in the way the mother was to do in her own era of worldly power.

Within this generic totem we can easily discern the god of the next developmental stage, who not only retained his non-material character, but also became even more perfect in the face of all attempts of ancient civilized peoples to concretize him until Christian myth finally reinstated all of his ancient spiritual meaning. From the esoteric connotation of totemism and matriarchy there is a direct path to Christianity which, of course, formulated the animistic characteristics of totemism into a religious dogma. As a psychological interpretation of totemism, Christianity not only proves that totemism was a spiritual belief, but also shows with what tenacity man adhered to the immortality of his soul. And it demonstrates again that we cannot fully understand spiritual phenomena unless we can incorporate later developmental forms into some synthetic and genetic comparison; the new not only preserves something of the old, but also represents a clearer version of it consciously produced by the pressure of growing psychological knowledge.

We can now appreciate more fully the development of Christianity from the substrata of Roman patriarchy and Jewish racial perpetuation. Christianity's overemphasis of the paternal role goes back to fecundation by the spirit, because this process guarantees immortality of the soul instead of just the race or people. Jesus himself was begotten by the Holy Ghost whose symbol, the dove, was an esoteric version of the ancient spirit bird. However, naturally conceived children carry the sins of the world, and they gain a soul only by baptism, which symbolizes the spiritual conception without which immortality is impossible.

A deeper basis for Christianity's attitude toward sexuality lies in this resurgence of esoteric spiritual belief. The Church had to extend primitive sexual restrictions into complete prohibition, for, under the assumptions of spiritual belief, sexual intercourse was not essential to reproduction, and was therefore sinful lust. Yet the seed—not the sperm or the egg, but the soul—which generates immortality as well as life, is just as effective for reproduction under totemism as under Christianity. In representing the generic soul of totemism, Christ personified the immortal soul, which role accounts for his thoroughly nonhuman traits. As soul he not only could

28

die and be resurrected, but his death and resurrection were the essential features of the soul, just as the immortal Double had copied the mortal bodily self.

This esoteric spiritual meaning explains not only Christ's accidental traits but also the content of the Christian belief which is symbolized in the legend of Christ, and formulated in dogma and exegesis. This meaning is expressed in its dependence on eternal life, and in life's being but a preparation for a death which introduces immortality and underlies it in a completely animistic sense. Yet more important than this and other parallels is another difference characteristic of this developmental stage. Although there is a direct path from totemistic belief to Christianity, we should not overlook the changes undergone by social institutions of various peoples from totemism to Roman civilization. The transition from post-totemistic matriarchy to patriarchy of the Roman state was completely revolutionary in nature, so that with its exaltation of the mother, its debasement of the father, and its spiritualization of the son, Christianity represents a quite new adaptation of old ideas to the changed shape of things. In its doctrine of the Trinity, which symbolized the identity of the Holy Ghost with the Father and Son, Christianity attempted a new synthesis which transcended totemism, mother-divinity, and patriarchy. For the first time, the son received the spiritual role which the mother had held under matriarchy and the father had held under the family-state. This final stage made possible the emergence of the *individual*, whom our modern democratic commonwealth recognizes as the product of matriarchy and paternal rule. This is the irreligious era of the rule of the child, which we shall discuss elsewhere.

However, speaking genetically, we detect in Christian

dogma a new and powerful attempt to save belief in the soul both from the materialism of the Roman father-state and from its concretion in the Jewish patriarchal family. Christian dogma states simply that one must believe, because on belief alone depend both the soul and the individual immortality which the Romans had traded for rule of the people, and the Jews had sold for the mess of pottage they honored as limitless reproduction and preservation of the family. When man puts his faith in his family or his state, and no longer believes in his individual soul or in the personal immortality symbolized by myth, cult, and dogma, he loses his higher values. All the bitter intra- and extra-mural strife of the Church has been nothing but humanity's inevitable attempt to preserve its ancient belief in the soul, which immortality esoterically symbolizes. In the course of such strife, the hostile powers of materialism and intellectuality became personified in the Devil, who represented the damned and departed soul, just as Christ who opposed him symbolized man's immortal soul. Only Christianity now symbolized the soul by the son, or, according to legalistic family organization, by an ever-recurring and realistic Double of the father. Thus the father made good his spiritual claim on the child only under a fully developed patriarchal family organization generated in post-exile Judaism and culminating in Roman law, because his son had now become his real Double for whom he would willingly sacrifice everything as long as his own name, rank, and office could be perpetuated.

Christianity's new version of religious belief in the soul inheres in the fact that, in man's undying struggle to save his own soul, Christian belief saved all our souls from annihilation and from the loss of their esoteric meaning which had been threatened by the intensified efforts of legal and

30

social institutions to make the soul materialistic and concrete. The success of such efforts would have meant the loss of belief in immortality, without which life would have had no purpose and value; otherwise man would not have fought and sacrificed for this belief as he has done now for centuries.

Yet the soul is always in just as great danger from the inflated, introspective knowledge of self which modern psychology has established as a science of understanding the "causal" motives of thinking, feeling, and action. As our first chapter contends, this knowledge is not a mere "natural science," but an eminently psychological, introspective, and interpretative knowledge. This psychological knowledge threatens purely spiritual values from within, just as the concretions of spiritual belief represented by family, state, and society threaten them from without. Psychology is the soul's worst enemy, because in creating its own consolation for death it becomes compelled by the self-knowledge it creates to prove that the soul does not exist. Thus it becomes both a scientific "psychology without a soul" and a kind of overburdening of the inner spiritual self which, with no support from an inherent belief in immortality, goes to pieces in a way the neuroses show so well.

In a materialistic age which suffered from self-awareness and threatened to forfeit its belief not only in immortality but also in religion, as the exoteric representative of such belief, psychoanalysis signified a new attempt to save the spiritual in man. The most remarkable feature of this attempt was the fact of its occurrence within the mentality of our time, for it not only provided an exoteric symbolization and social concretion for the soul concept of earlier epochs, but it also tried to establish this concept in the manner of a natural science. Yet this kind of realistic psychology could only mean the death of the soul, whose origin, being, and worth inhered necessarily in the abstract, the ineffable, and the esoteric. The initial appeal of psychoanalysis to man may be explained by its attempt to prove that his lost soul existed again; but man's final resistance to it is explained by its attempt to develop such proof by a scientific method. This kind of proof had to fail, because all it could do was to show that it could no more prove the existence of the soul scientifically than it could similarly prove the existence of God, with whom the soul is identified. In all scientific attempts to prove its existence, the soul has evaporated just like the noble metals in the alchemist's retort, which finally held not the substance hoped for, but only the residues of baser elements. Even in psychoanalysis man has tried to hold fast to that which he really needed and wanted, for he has looked to this "psychology without a soul" for a doctrine of salvation which it could never provide, even though its therapy echoed the idea of salvation. After all, therapy works only as long as it can sustain man's ancient illusory belief in the soul, and only when it can offer him a soul without psychology.

PSYCHOLOGY
AND THE SEXUAL ERA

> *Not for one conquest alone does*
> *Helen have all of Pandora's charms.*
>
> BACHOFEN

O‌UR OUTLINE OF THE DEVELOP-
ment of the soul concept from primitive belief in immortality
suggests that sexuality was more restricted in primitive life
than in antiquity or modern times. Even primitives, whom
ethnologists regard as nonreligious, maintained firm social
organizations and close regulation of sex. If cultures as
primitive as these involved sexual restrictions, it is no wonder
that the hypothesis of original promiscuity has not been
substantiated by recorded history. This hypothesis characterized the evolutionary thought of our preceding century
and its comparison of man with animals. But a closer study
of the animal world, and of higher apes in particular, shows
that many animals are monogamous, or that they are at
least more restrictive in sexual relations than the term promiscuity would connote.[1] And the hypothesis of primitive

[1] See the unusually comprehensive study by G. S. Miller, Jr., "Some Elements
of Sexual Behavior in Primates, and Their Possible Influence on the Beginnings of Human Social Development." *Journal of Mammalogy*, Vol. 9, No.
4, Nov. 1928. On animal life in general, see Fr. Alverdes, *Animal Psychology* (Tierpsychologie), Leipzig, 1925.

promiscuity can scarcely rest on any wish to restore this appealing state of affairs, because historical tradition shows no evidence of such a fantasy. Even contemporary experience can teach us that promiscuity yields no greater individual happiness than did the rigid sexual tabus of primitive cultures.

On the basis of my own studies I am inclined to believe that human sex life did not develop from a primal state of promiscuity into one of restraint, but from a sex life which was restricted biologically by rutting, and psychologically by spiritual belief, into a greater sexual freedom for the individual. At a certain stage of human evolution there occurred what one may call the discovery of sexuality. The ensuing "sexual era" succeeded a more primitive one that had been dominated by the stress of living and the threat of death. As I shall try to show, this primitive era had been characterized by a naïve belief in immortality of the self, from which a dawning sense of death had produced the compensatory idea of an immortal body-soul preserved as the ego's Double. What I have called the discovery of sexuality followed a painful relinquishment of individual immortality, which was precipitated by the further recognition of death inherent in man's unwilling acceptance of sexuality as a means of conquering death through procreative survival.

Sex and reproduction were sharply distinguished by primitive man. He believed that reproduction was mediated not by sexual intercourse, but by entrance of the soul of the dead into the body of woman, who then effected rebirth and immortality of the soul. Therefore sexual tabus were not restrictions, but expressions of man's inherent belief in his

34

individual immortality; and it is in this way that primitive sexual regulation differed favorably from our own.

Jewish-Christian doctrine turned the complete identification of sex and reproduction into a religious dogma which modern science has interpreted causally. We find this causal interpretation expanded in the faulty psychoanalytic conclusion that sex plays the primary psychological role because of its biological primacy. Yet the place of sex in human history follows neither from its original biological role in reproduction nor from its ultimate psychological role in love, but from its spiritual role which substituted procreative for individual immortality.

In antiquity the role of sexuality culminated in religious mysteries and cosmic sexual myths in which the soul and sexuality had much the same meaning. Christianity separated the soul from sexuality again, because by that time the sensual significance of sex had come to outweigh its biological and spiritual aspects. This observation naturally suggests only the bare outline of what I mean, for any given stage of conscious development involves the interaction and successive dominance of many factors. For example, the primitive world picture dominated by an egocentric wish for individual immortality never fades from man's spiritual history, although the subsequent ideologies of sexuality and modern science formally exclude it. And, on the other hand, the beginnings of the sexual era and natural science causality are present even in certain primitive rites and myths. In spite of these overlapping phenomena we may say, speaking spiritually, that the primitive view, dominated by the idea of death, has persistently and consistently tried to preserve individual immortality. This effort, which is particularly

35

characteristic of such social institutions as religion, morals, and community relationships, appears in the ancient world, and especially in Egyptian culture. In Greece the conflict ended with the hero's victory over the gods and divine law, and with the final, tragic downfall of the hero as a self-established superman. The Roman Empire embodied a complete social or legal recognition of sex as the means to reproductive immortality, just as the Jews had recognized it religiously. In opposition to the extreme Roman concretion of spirituality which threatened belief in individual immortality, Christianity tried to unite individual immortality, and sexuality as the means thereto, into its characteristic glorification of the child or son. Rite and eschatology then added individual immortality of the soul to a much greater extent than before, because the soul in and of itself could now become immortal without first having to enter the child at the time of conception. The doctrine of immaculate conception, in which both of these means to immortality seem united, is paralleled by the Egyptian identification of the soul with the corporeal Double, or Ka, that made embalming a guarantee of individual immortality. At the same time, the religious and social esteem of woman, which symbolized her acceptance in terms of reproductive immortality, produced the concept of reincarnation embodied in the myth of Osiris and the cult of Isis as forerunners of Christianity. Here also was anchored the idea of incest, which was an attempt to unite within the self both the individual and reproductive types of immortality which resulted from the self's entering and being born again by the mother. At a later time this new version of personal immortality was rejected as being too individualistic, and the individual was left only with such collective means for satisfying his claim to immortality as religion, morals, and marital sexuality. The tendency on the part of strong-willed individuals to acquire a personal immortality in excess of their fair share recurred in cults and pacts with the Devil, which incidentally were celebrated by incestuous rites.

Belief in individual immortality is so much a part of the self that, although religious, sexual, and social organizations provide collective substitutes for individual immortality, the individual constantly seeks to perpetuate his ego and his self in individual works. In the last three chapters of the present volume we shall consider the individual's uncompromising tendencies towards immortality in his dreams, his living, and his works, all as phenomena of will. I think it is important to bring out the fundamental opposition between the individual will, which seeks to perpetuate itself, and the collective soul, which is immortal, and to show that both are in great degree united in sexuality. Why they are denied as means of salvation more often than before is a problem for our ensuing discussion.

Primitive man's attitude during the presexual era clearly indicates that sexuality meant something *inner*, and not something as realistic as a relation with the opposite sex. This view is confirmed by a further study of primitive man, which upsets another prejudice of evolutionary history. Ethnologists now recognize that, unlike our own world, primitive man's world was magical and not realistic. That is, everything real was involved in the primitive's ego and determined by it. In contrast we have created a reality closely corresponding to ourselves, yet which we still know and signify as an *outer* technological or moral world. Thus we feel ourselves inhibited by all kinds of *outer* restrictions which our egos actually create within themselves for their

37

own salvation, while primitive man simply accepted these restrictions as parts of himself (tabus). In the presexual era, sex meant something spiritual rather than a means of reproduction or a source of pleasure. But this spiritual significance of sex meant that the individual might lose his immortality at the time his soul entered the child. Our so-called neurotics manifest a corresponding, basic anxiety or fear of death because of their too blind adherence to the egoistic belief in immortality which mankind has never really given up and probably never can. Sexual resistance (anxiety) is natural to the individual; it comes from within and not from without; it is egoistic and not moralistic; and, in the sense of primitive, presexual immortality belief, it signifies a fear of death. As long as sexuality is not accepted as a means to immortality, it threatens the self. This is shown by spontaneous feelings of fear and guilt in children who have no other reason for such feelings, and by adults' guilt and fear regarding their own sexual behavior, which Freud has described as "actual neuroses." We know now that no external "threat of castration" first evokes these anxiety reactions, but that they arise spontaneously. We have misunderstood them heretofore, and have explained them by reference to external "causes," but they may only be understood spiritually and in relation to the magical and noncausal ideology from which they emerged.

In this sense the religious-social organizations of primitives do not restrict the individual sexually, but rather make possible for him that sexual life which he has always been neurotically ready to sacrifice for the sake of his personal immortality. In the same sense, marriage made sex possible for man of the sexual era because it recognized sex and justified it religiously as a means to reproductive immortality. Thus spiritual belief explains not the sexual resistance encountered in neurotics and all others, but the conquest of such resistance and the transition from the era of the self, with its naïve belief in immortality, to the era of sex which accepted reproductive immortality and sexuality as its means. As follows from our previous explanations, this transition was effected by spiritual belief, and was only a renewed attempt to salvage as much of man's diminishing belief in individual immortality as possible.

We now encounter the first paradox in the development of this problem, which is replete with crises, reversals, and contradictions. The naïve disjunction of sexuality and reproduction, which is characteristic of primitive stages of the presexual era, still remains valid in the feeling life of man, in spite of all efforts of religion, morality, and science to restore their relationship. It is only the psychic significance of sex and reproduction which changes at the various developmental stages of the individual or race. Under the primitive world view, in which spirits of the dead effected impregnation independently of the sex act, intercourse was a natural act of pleasure to which man gave himself under certain circumstances and at certain times. In the sexual era this naïve, playful, sexual activity became tabu, and the sex act was restricted to impregnation for the sake of begetting children and achieving reproductive immortality. In primitive times the sex act was not concerned with reproduction, because reproduction threatened individual immortality; but in the sexual era it *had* to concern reproduction, which was the only current means of insuring reproductive immortality. It now seems possible to understand man's longing for an ostensibly primal sexual freedom as an inclination to recapture his naïve belief in immortality, which

39

such longing signifies. But this sexual freedom was only a negative accretion to the primitive point of view, whose positive side had distinguished sexuality from impregnation and reproduction. Thus, even in the contemporary neurotic type of person, the longing for sexual freedom is just a demand for freedom in general and for liberation from the fetters of regulated reproduction (marriage), for when the neurotic is offered a chance to satisfy his wish, his desire disappears. Hence the fear of loss of self in physical death and in the psychic sense of immortality automatically regulates sexual activity and avenges with fear and guilt each misuse of sex for the sake of the individual alone. Even the neurasthenic's professed cause (post-ejaculatory weakness) of his sexual malaise seems to be only an echo of the individual's ancient concern for his own immortality, for like modern athletes, primitive man abstained from sexual intercourse in order to conserve his strength.

Before we pursue the psychic implications of conscious and deliberate abstention from sexual intercourse and trace its profound changes during man's history, we must consider the sex drive as such in so far as it is manifested independently of reproduction and the sex act. We know, for example, that the so-called "perversions," which Freud has described as gratification tendencies inhering in the sex drive, derive meaning from spiritual belief. Perversions played a quite insignificant role in primitive times, in contrast with early and late antiquity. While impregnation by animals was a purely spiritual matter in primitive times, the Egyptian Amon cult materialized this spiritual concept in the bull of Heliopolis which fertilized woman, or Hathor, the celestial cow. The same concretion of the animal as soul-bearer appears in the Creto-Mycenean minotaur. In Grecian legend it was the Jovian bull that eloped with Europa. After Alexandria this cult penetrated Hellenism as the "holy union" *(hieros gamos),* and under Gnostic practices it degenerated into a sexual orgy. However, the idea of potency, which appears to have originated in the cult of the bull, implies a spiritual rather than a physical power. This power is the "mana" which was transformed later into the god, priest, or king.

From animal cults we find it an easy step to animal sacrifice, in which eating of the sacrifice again signified an acquisition of secret energy with which man could impregnate woman without losing any of his own power. The eating of meat which modern dietetics justifies on a chemical basis was pursued by primitive man on a magical basis, just as many magical discoveries have been found to be justifiable on other bases. The eating of human flesh and blood is symbolic even for cannibals, just as the body of Christ symbolizes the individual Christian's share in the universal soul. Nourishment has always been a matter of ingesting the spiritual substance believed to exist in every living thing. The specific, sexual meaning of such eating is so widespread even today that it is to be regarded as "perverse" only from the standpoint of a cannibalistic state which has a *social* conception of collective immortality.[1a] In the rites of certain Gnostic sects, and to some extent in Middle Age cults of the devil, the eating of human sperm evolved into formal semen cults. The intent of such a procedure was to avoid the misuse of semen in fertilization by literally fertilizing

[1a] I have suggested ideas similar to these in my work "Perversion and Neurosis" (Perversion und Neurose), *Zeitschrift für Psychoanalyse,* VIII, 1922; in English in the *International Journal of Psychoanalysis,* IV, 1923. Reprinted in the separately published volume *Sexuality and Guilt* (Sexualität und Schuldgefühl), 1926.

oneself through the process of swallowing. As another escape from sexual to individual immortality, it was more radical than the incest allied with Gnostic and devil cults. Oral fertilization of woman, which appeared only in sexualized spiritual beliefs of antiquity and not in primitive spiritual belief, was only a derivative of self-fertilization, which had also been economical of semen. As the biblical "breath of life" signifies, oral fertilization itself was allied with the breath. However, not only the origin of, but the continued adherence to, these relationships in folklore, fairy tales, and childish beliefs[2] is explained by the naïve concept of the soul and by man's hopeless resistance to giving up his doctrine of immortality. The issue has always been one of immortality and of the salvation of man's soul from dissipation under the sexual era's ideology of fertilization. Ignorance of the relation between intercourse and fertilization was as completely irrelevant to the problems of conception and perversion as it is with our own children. But one must still explain the stability of this relation once it was recognized, as it must have been in antiquity. In folklore and among adults we find just a reverse action in which the individual consciously sought and perpetuated these "perversions" because the sexual era had accepted the relationship between intercourse and fertilization. Under a sexual point of view, perversions offered the individual a chance to cheat the world of his share of immortality, which enables us to understand both the social bans placed on these practices and the

[2] See my *Socio-psychological Parallels to Children's Theories of Sexuality* (Völkerpsychologische Parallelen zu den infantilen Sexualtheorien), 1911. The kiss may well derive its significance from spiritual belief in oral fertilization. Perhaps the Italian proverb, *Donna basata mezza ciavada*, can be interpreted as follows: the kiss is the real agent of fertilization; the coitus that follows it is a mere formality.

42

individual guilt-feelings which inevitably accompanied them. Adherence to such "infantile" sexual theories and practices rests on their spiritual and not their libidinal meanings, and they survived because they made individual spiritual belief more tenable in the face of an accepted sexual point of view. It would be interesting to determine the extent to which perversions originated in spiritual belief, for it seems beyond question that perversions served spiritual ends in certain ancient cults and ideologies. Even the homosexuality of the Greeks seems more comprehensible on such a basis. When the sexual era was at its height in Greece, woman played a proportionately exalted role as mother. However, in the sense of her prevailing spiritual belief, woman still stood outside sexuality and was fertilized by a god and not by man. Accordingly, a man sought both to protect his soul and to gratify his senses with a hetaira who was not a mother. Boy-love expressed a respect not so much for sex as for its product, the son, in whom the real self and the real soul survived. Christianity spiritualized this idea by deifying the son. But in Greek boy-love, which represented a "spiritual friendship," the adult sought to impress his self, his own spirit, his real soul upon the beloved youth. In this phenomenon there lies the deep relationship of so-called homosexuality to narcissism, which psychoanalysis discovered and which still echoes this "negative" or neurotic homosexuality in the Double. In boy-love, man fertilized both spiritually and otherwise the living image of his own soul, which seemed materialized in an ego as idealized and as much like his own body as was possible. In emphasizing the soul and not sex in their boy-love (see the discussion of the study of Psyche, page 49), the Greeks achieved unique status among peoples of the sexual era.

The sexual era involved a man-made world or world view which had been characteristic of primitive times. I say world view, because peoples as well as individuals live by ideologies and perish from their imperfections. Ideologies are expressions of life power and represent attitudes toward life and its basic facts. The actual external collapse of a people or of an individual follows a gradual undermining of its ideology, which can be valid only for a time. An ideational breakdown often precedes the real one for so long a period that the causal connection generally goes unnoticed, and the individual or people goes on mechanically living off its spiritual capital, which soon gives out if it is not replenished with a new ideology.

The primitive world view included *man* and *his* immortality. As shown by the Dirne theme, *woman's* social inferiority followed from her spiritual imperfections. In the sexual era woman began to overcome what had always been a man-made world view. In Egypt, where embalming and spiritual cults involving fertilization by the totem conflicted with cults of sexual reincarnation, woman first achieved a matriarchal and spiritual status which recurred in the Christian cult of Mary the Mother. Cults of the Devil, which denied sexuality as a means to immortality, debased woman from this lofty belief in immortality and the soul to the accursed status she bore under witchcraft.

Before we cite several traditions which show the transformation undergone by spiritual belief from the ancient sexual era to the Christian era of the child, we ought to review the naïve era of the self in order to identify more clearly the basic, primitive, spiritual tendency in all its changing forms. According to the original belief, woman was fertilized not by man but by a spirit through which the soul of a dead ancestor sought rebirth. We have seen that woman herself finally assumed this animating role, from which man then tried to eject her because it made her a threat to his personal immortality. Man's attitude was the relatively simple one of denying his role of progenitor as long as he could, and of refusing it when denial became impossible. Of course he did not consciously and deliberately reject this role at first, for, according to the original belief, fertilization was independent of sexual intercourse. It was the growing difficulty of maintaining this naïve spiritual belief during the sexual era that led to man's deliberate abstinence from sexual intercourse. This difficulty grew out of the recognition that procreation was dangerous to the individual and his immortality. Then woman's role came to the fore, and became more significant and more complicated as time went on.

We need only to consider a few traditions in order to appreciate this crucial change and its effect on woman. In the Book of Tobit we recognize the ancient if not primitive tradition of the night of chastity. This legend relates how the evil spirit Asmodi killed seven fiancés on the eve of their intended marriages to Sarah. Finally God's emissary, Tobias, succeeded in breaking the spell, obviously by abstaining from sexual intercourse and seduction by the Devil as the other seven candidates had not done. Other more recent legends based on this theme showed that when the husband abstained from intercourse on the first night, he died, and so succumbed to the spell of the wicked spirit in whom the ancient spiritual meaning seemed reversed. In these later traditions woman also seemed to play the more active role, which had been latent in the Tobias saga; for even though one accepts the psychoanalytic interpretation that the jealous father who dug his daughter's grave thereby invoked her death, it was woman who was fundamentally guilty of man's death. This guilt was generated by the loss of the man's soul during his exposure to the hazards of intercourse. Also, the father's wish to keep his own daughter for himself was anchored in spiritual belief and, like the incest-wish, it indicated his attempt to preserve his personal immortality in his child in spite of sexuality. A pervasive custom seems to have verified this basic spiritual belief more clearly than has the sexualized history of incest.[3] According to Reitzenstein,[4] the kernel of this tradition is that the daughter of a sonless father can be reared as a son, and marries only the man who subdues and wins her in combat. The suitor must then be made à member of the family by the ceremony usually reserved for women. This idea doubtless originated with the sonless father who wanted to survive in his daughter. In the spiritual era his desire was symbolized by the daughter's masculinization, and in the sexual era by the father's incestuous relations with her. In such primitive groups as the peninsular Malayans, the Battas of Sumatra, and the Alfuros of Celebes, where the father is the first to live with his daughter, the father not only preserves his own soul in his daughter but by impregnating her beforehand saves the soul of the future man who takes her as his wife. Later traditions depict the daughter and not the father as the one who sets the terms for winning her. These requirements were usually tests of strength and wit which had the esoteric objective of subduing her sexually on the first night. In the Tobias saga woman's role was pas-

---

[3] Rank: *The Incest Motif* (Das Inzest-Motiv), 2nd ed., chap. 6.
[4] F. Reitzenstein: *Woman among Primitive Peoples* (Das Weib bei den Naturvölkern), Berlin, 1923.

sive; here it was active. Yet in both of these situations man's fate depended on his attitude toward sex in the sense of the old spiritual belief. In the Tobias saga man died because he yielded to sexual temptation and lost his own soul as progenitor. In the later traditions he died when he adhered to the old custom of abstinence and refused to accept the new sexual world view which woman represented. Woman now demanded of him those qualities of strength and courage which had previously characterized the fructifying god. In this phase of the sexual era man had to overcome the sexual anxiety rooted in his spiritual belief and in its implications of immortality. His contention with the strong Brünhilde type of woman really comprised a victory over his own masculine anxiety and not over the sexual resistance of woman, on whom he seemed only to be projecting his inhibition. This projection may also account for the masculine character of many of those heroines who resist only in so far as they are obliged to mirror masculine resistance, and it may have something to do with the fact that the father often made his daughter's subjugation harder by his own masculine psychology, which inclined him to identify with the suitor. In any event, in conformance with the father's desire, the daughter had masculine traits inconsistent with any Oedipus role, because her father's wish was founded in spiritual belief.

Unless we can translate the language of the sexual era into that of the spiritual era, we cannot understand even the biological facts of sex. Just as masculine sexual anxiety was projected as feminine sex resistance, man's abstention from intercourse with a menstruating woman seems to have been only a realistic excuse for his resistance. There is no biological justification for such resistance, since woman is more

47

receptive to sex and fertilization during menstruation than at other times.[5] Menstruation only offered the anxiety-ridden man a welcome excuse to shrink from the danger inherent in woman. The same principle applies to the "virginity tabu," Freud's insightful explanation of which beautifully illustrates the denial of spiritual concepts by masculine psychologizing.[6]

Although man's anxieties in all these legends of his "night of trial" still derive from threats to the well-being of his soul, we must not forget that woman was his seducer and a counterpart of the serpent in Eden. The serpent was cursed along with Eve, but it also symbolized man's sexual excitement, and it could carry both of these roles because it had once been an animating spirit animal. However, woman's seductive acts were valuable to the man because they allowed him to forget his soul long enough to perform his necessary sexual function. And perhaps woman had deeper and more practical motives which enabled her to move the man to lay aside his inhibitions, for man had to recognize his spiritual fatherhood, which his difficult acceptance of sexual immortality had made possible. Woman naturally had little trouble accepting the principle of sexual immortality, since the child in a way guaranteed her own immortality. But then, in her first efforts to emancipate herself from masculine spiritual belief which the sexual point of view was

---

[5] Perhaps the number of nights of chastity (3-4) during which the husband had to abstain corresponds to the average menstrual period.

[6] Even the cutting off of the clitoris, which Spencer and Gillen have described in Central Australian tribes as a fertility charm and preparation for sexual intercourse, seems to be a substitute for defloration and to correspond to fertilization by another man. Perhaps even the idea of circumcision is related to the spiritual significance of blood, just as the blood covenant is based on a spiritual relationship. On the basis of spiritual belief, virginity is meaningless. It was important only in the sexual area, as a guarantee of a man's possession of his wife and child.

beginning to displace, she had no easy time establishing herself as the official bearer of the soul. In a long struggle, which the Milesian tale of Psyche beautifully symbolizes, woman became the spiritual as well as the biological representative of reproductive sexuality. The story of Psyche portrays the spiritualization of sexuality which had originated in antiquity, was interrupted by the ecclesiastical disjunction of these two elements, began to acquire a religious significance in love songs of the Middle Ages, and finally culminated in romantic love. Modern science biologized both the soul and sex; our contemporary love psychology then did away with the soul.

From the outset, sexual knowledge played a decisive role in this evolution. In all legends from that of the Fall through Sin to fairy tales, the recognition of sex, which spiritual and sexual man consistently rejected, appears as a curse fulfilled by death and the loss of immortality. Psyche's recognition of her spouse, who appeared as totem animal and invisible spirit, brought pain and death to his human form. Recognition of her partner's spiritual significance helped him to win immortality, but her recognition of his sexual significance robbed him of his immortality. In this connection the common heroic motif of pseudoinsanity may be interpreted as a denial of sexual knowledge whose recognition would have threatened the hero's soul. A case in point was Peronnik, the prototype of the fool Parsifal, who used "naïveté" to escape sexual seduction and to win the Grail as a symbol of immortality.[7] His successor, Lohengrin,[8] who tried to conceal his human role by insisting that women were insoluble

---

[7] See Victor Junk: Saga and Poetry of the Grail in the Middle Ages (Gralsage und Graldichtung des Mittelalters), Vienna, 1912.

[8] Rank: The Lohengrin Saga. A Contribution to the Form and Meaning of its Motif. (Die Lohengrinsage. Ein Beitrag zu ihrer Motivgestaltung und Deutung), Vienna, 1911.

puzzles, was the clever type of hero whose ability consisted not in solving the sexual puzzle but in saving himself from its spiritual dangers in spite of his sexual knowledge.

A typical development of this whole system of ideas has been preserved in the Turandot saga. In this story it was not the father who posed the problems for his daughter's suitors, but the daughter herself who did it in the face of opposition from her father, Turan (Turan-doht means Turan's daughter). She set a problem calling for ingenuity rather than physical strength, Prince Kalaf's solution of which greatly pleased the king and his entire court because so many suitors of the cruel princess had already lost their lives trying to solve it. The important feature of this legend was the prince's sympathy for the conquered princess, which he showed by his agreement to postpone the marriage night on the condition that she guess his name and descent by the following morning. The prince also resisted seduction by Turandot's slaves, who wanted to unlock "the secret of the future" for him. His postponement and resistance again betray man's motive to abstain on the first night, at a stage at which the father no longer struggled[9] against his daughter's suitors, but with them against her. Men joined against woman's first efforts to emancipate herself from masculine spiritual belief, for Turandot struggled not only against her suitor but against her father, who justified his control over her by spiritual belief. And in her suitor she contested her

---

[9] In the Latin history of Appollonius of Tyre, King Antioch offered his daughter's suitors a puzzle which symbolized his incestuous relations with her. Another Persian princess asked her suitor a question relating to her secret amour with a hateful sorcerer whom she kept hidden in a subterranean chamber, and to whom she had borne two children (Haxthausen; Transkaukasia, 1, 326). Here again the invisible (secret) and bestial (hateful) procreator is opposed to the legitimate swain.

father, or the new father-right of the sexual era, which robbed her of certain freedoms and merely transferred her from the domination of her father to that of her lover, spouse, and fructifier.

Although they correspond to another cultural stage, similar motifs can be detected in the Grecian saga of Helen, which illustrates the marital version of the daughter's struggle for sexual freedom. As mentioned before,[10] Helen manifests the last traces of woman's matriarchal status and fraternal group marriage, which ethnologists since Morgan have regarded as a universal developmental stage in sexual life, and which many have considered as the primal form of marriage (polyandry).[11] The present instance concerns the marriage of a group of brothers to one woman, as shown by the myth of Helen and the related Trojan sagas. In the latter we find Castor and Pollux,[12] who avenged Helen's abduction on Theseus; Agamemnon, who was inseparable from his brother's wife and was finally slain by his own wife and her lover; and finally the Trojan brothers, of whom Paris was Helen's legitimate abductor. According to similar legends, Helen herself had belonged to still other brothers, one of whom was Deiphobus. What is of interest here is the notorious conflict in Hellenic mythology between the old spiritual pattern of group marriage devoid of physical fatherhood, and the emergent patriarchy of the sexual era in which the husband dominated woman because he alone possessed and fertilized her. Matriarchal woman had belonged to no

[10] See a study of the epic, planned since 1917, which echoes this primitive relationship.

[11] See the psychological critique of corresponding ethnological material in Chapter 8 of my book: *The Incest Motif in Poetry and Saga* (Das Inzest-Motiv in Dichtung und Sage), 2nd edit., 1926.

[12] *Op. cit.*, p. 424.

51

one man, because she bore both the collective soul or totem and the attendant religious and social prestige which she struggled so to preserve in the sexual era.

The concurrent change in man's status may be characterized briefly. Man had originally borne only the sexual role, because fertilization had been reserved for the functioning soul-bearer, spirit, totem, or god. The sexual era masculinized woman or the mother as soul-bearer, and in so doing gave her such a preferred social and religious matriarchal status that man became compelled to do something about his own immortality, whose naïve basis sexual knowledge had destroyed. The failure of the matriarchal system to provide man with a procreative substitute in his child apparently compelled him to relinquish his sexual resistance and to recognize his role as fructifier in order to insure procreative immortality for himself in his child. But in doing this he had to insure his fatherhood, so that he demanded sole possession of the woman again. And since she could see no gain for herself in this new order, she proceeded to battle for her old rights. If for no other reason than this, she rejected man as a substitute for the fructifying god whose place he was trying to usurp. In the light of this analysis, many conflicts of Greek heroes reduce to tests of the man's power in which he sought to legitimatize his divine role, though in some of these instances it was the woman herself who brought about the man's downfall (*cf.* Hercules).[12a]
For example, Paris appears in the traditional role of divine fructifier, although Homer held him up as a weakling against the masculine spouse of Menelaus. The later saga softened the abduction of the god, in the judgment of Paris. This

[12a] As we shall show in our discussion of the Gilgamesh epic (see p. 105), this is a typical motif in man's struggle against the emerging sexual era.

corresponds to the ingenious decision of the riddle solver who, in the sense of ancient spiritual belief, decided in favor of illegitimate fructification (Venus) and against the goddess of marriage (Juno). Helen, the progeny of Leda and the swan (spirit-bird), represented the immortal soul incarnate in matriarchal woman, about whom raged the battles of men, heroes, and gods.

Let us turn to our major problems and to Christianity, which should tell us much about the influence of spiritual belief in the soul upon the nature and decline of the sexual era. As I have shown in an earlier work,[13] under Christianity's influence the Don Juan material treats sexuality spiritually rather than physically. As a special character, to be sure, Don Juan was the last of the heroic types to retain the right of "first possession of the woman" in the sense of ancient spiritual belief qualified by Christian antisexuality.

With this in mind, let us consider Don Juan's relation to man, woman, and himself. As is the case with all divine, spiritual fructifiers, Don Juan's relation to man was not that of a rival; he would not kill a man in order to win a woman, because by his very nature he was above having sexual rivals. His natural opponent was woman, whom he conquered by craftiness rather than by strength of personality. A similar motif from the Greek Amphytrion saga concerns the search for amorous pleasure while masquerading as a legitimate lover (spouse) in the callous fashion of Don Juan. And just like the god in this saga who was confident of victory over any mortal spouse, Don Juan competed as a husband's superior. The legitimate lover was absolutely essential to the Don Juan character, whose characteristic act was not to ex-

---

[13] "The Don Juan Character" (Die Don Juan Gestalt), *Imago*, 1922; Sep. 1924.

clude or supplant the lover but to rob and betray him. This was obviously a new version of the ancient spiritual belief on the basis of which a strong-willed superman justified his right to fructify woman spiritually and to supplant the totem or deity. With the changed attitude toward this ancient right, the "hero" became obliged to conquer the man by power and the woman by craft, so that the hero whose function had been sacred evolved into an instrument of frivolity.

A closer examination seems to alter the usual meaning of Don Juan's relation to women. He wanted not so much just to reach his sexual goal, of which he felt both certain and deserving, but to reach it in the way and under the circumstances described above, for it was only a woman with a legitimate husband who stimulated him. This was not because of a wife's allure in the sense of Freud's "damaged third," but because Don Juan's role required him to take advantage of the husband. Don Juan's premarital relations with a woman already promised to another implied absolutely nothing about fatherhood, but signified rather the role of a totem or animating deity. Don Juan wanted the woman just once and not forever. The Romanticists who worked over the Don Juan material went so far with their poetic motivation of his character as to liken him to the Devil, who tempts the body less than the spirit.

It seems to me that this motivation involves something of the old spiritual belief whose Christianized elements underlie the whole Don Juan material and his relation to the Romantic character of Faust, the master of the black arts, and not their docile scholar. Goethe, who had preceded the Romanticists, had made Faust a sublime wrestler with self and truth by projecting his infernal traits on an externalized tempter, while Don Juan actually symbolized the Devil, and his human traits were split off into a servant-Double.[14] This assimilation, or identification, of Don Juan and the Devil seems so obvious that one wonders why the poets did not come closer to understanding the material inhering in their allusions. The explanation for their failure may well lie in the fact that man knew very little about the Devil, and it might even turn out that Don Juan could tell us more about him than could the Church, once Don Juan's identity with him and its relation to spiritual belief were recognized.

If Don Juan were to tell one less about the Devil than one already believed one knew it might even seem that the Devil personified an uninhibited impulse-life with an emphasis on sexuality. But once we regard the Devil as a precipitate of the sexual era which Christian belief had overthrown, his obvious relation to the immortal soul of ancient spiritual belief becomes understandable. Although the Church freed the soul from the clutches of sexuality, the fact that it also proclaimed the doctrines of spiritual fertilization and the soul's immortality stamped divine fertilization of the spirit as illicit and diabolical intercourse. Thus the Devil came to personify both a rejected sexuality opposed to personal immortality, and a mortal, sexualized, and damned soul opposed to the immortal self which was symbolized by the Christian God inherent in the resurrected Son. The spiritual God was obliged to assume certain features from the sexual era in order to exist at all, but such animal traits of the older spiritual gods as horns, a tail, and a cloven hoof were then attributed to the Devil because they were incompatible with the newer views. Thus the Devil represented a conception of the soul which Christian belief in immortality had shorn of sexuality, just as God represented a spiritualized conception of procreative immortal-

[14] See my study of Don Juan.

ity, so that the two roles were then completely reversed. During the sexual era fertilization by spirits of the dead had been sexualized by the recognition of fatherhood, while in Christianity sexual fertilization was stamped as sensuous pleasure.

We encounter all these stages of spiritual belief in Don Juan, who likewise embodied both the ancient, divine, fertilizing hero, and the sexuality which Christian belief had damned as mortal. We have now only to fit the role of woman into this relationship in order to revive our earlier theme. We found woman resisting her father's claims at the beginning of the sexual era, and contending with her equally demanding husband at a later stage. In Don Juan she now opposed her lover and fructifier who had been her ally in the myth of Helen. In order to understand this reversal of woman's attitude we need to consider the heterosexual love which Christianity initiated. In primitive man's progressively despiritualized world, and in the godless world of antiquity from which Christianity had developed, every man finally became a worldly proxy for the fructifying deity, and every woman a bearer and keeper of the soul. In other words, husband and wife as earthly personifications of the spiritual soul became spiritualizing agents not only of their child but of one another. In this development one may hopefully look for the origin of spiritual love and for an understanding of its remnants in fairy tales of the Psyche type, in which the hero or heroine was able to animate either the bewitched animal or the soulless beloved as long as its human character remained unrecognized.

In the "true character" of Don Juan, woman struggled over this spiritual love and the recognition of its spiritual laws. As a sexual and diabolical hero, Don Juan fell short of his role of divine animator, and at this stage of moral and social development he cheated the woman as well as the child. Such treason against the soul was condemned by man as well as woman. In the sense of this feminine ideology, every hero of a Don Juan legend met his downfall with the very first love to whom he was "untrue," just because he still owed her his soul. On the basis of the old beliefs, man wanted to refrain from fructification even though such abstinence would cost him his soul, which needed a feminine ideology to survive. Yet woman had no reason to dissuade the man she first possessed from a belief which would be useful to him were she to have him permanently, so that the Don Juan material portrays woman's second attempt to free herself from the bonds of sexualized spiritual belief. This attempt was turned not against the father and husband, as in the instances of Helen and Turandot, but against the illegitimate fructifier whose primal spiritual role had become diabolical, and against the "lover" who was a vulgarized "divine" fructifier of the sexual era. It is the spiritual role of such a fructifier, and not the "psychology of sex," which explains so many baffling "triangles."

This reversal of the sexual relationship which is so significant for our own society goes back to man-made spiritual belief, from whose gradual change and decline woman derived the greater benefit. Since it originally had been not only a duty but a religious honor for woman to be fertilized by the divine soul before giving herself to mortal man, a new moral evaluation resulted both from man's adherence to this custom which preserved his idea of immortality, and from woman's growing opposition to it. Pre- and extra-marital intercourse sustained man's tacitly guarded right to maintain his illegitimatized spiritual belief, but it antagonized the woman as mother. Just as such privileged classes of men as priests, kings, or heroes had once been sexual instruments of the divine soul, a tabued class of woman now became witches and harlots, or mere instruments of carnal satisfaction. This was a complete spiritual and moral reëvaluation of the old views that had been founded in spiritual belief. For men had previously been divided into two classes, one of which had a special *spiritual* power to fertilize woman premaritally, and the other could only use sexual intercourse to the same end. Now women fell into two classes, one of which served men hetairically in the sense of his superseded spiritual belief, and the other, as mothers, gave themselves to man in the sense of the new sexual ideology of the soul.

❋   ❋   ❋

In considering Don Juan as a humanized Devil we have gone beyond the sexual concretion of primitive spiritual belief characteristic of our own psychological era. Humanized spiritual representatives had been prominent in all rites and cults, from the primitive dance and sacrifice to Greek tragedy, and had found their ultimate dramatic and tragic expression in the life of Christ. The era of the drama produced a new form, for Don Juan, who symbolized an accursed sexual ideology and Devil, implied an effort to explain and motivate the soul's otherwise incomprehensible psychological qualities by portraying its ancient symbol in a form that was humanized as well as human. This ascription of human motives reflected the spirit of the times which the dramatist portrayed consciously, as well as his unconscious portrayed the ancient spirituality.

About the time the drama of Don Juan appeared in witch-ridden Spain, Elizabethan drama was at its height in Eng-

land. For us Shakespearian drama was a lofty art of psychological characterization. A closer scrutiny of this art discloses
a humanized version of the mythical and historical materials
that had appeared in earlier novels and dramas. Shakespeare
ascribed palpable motives to these traditional characters, because their old spiritual meanings had been lost; and since he
interpreted spiritual motives in terms of character types, he
appears to have been the first Western psychologist to achieve
a scientific psychological doctrine and characterology. For
the moment I cannot utterly prove what I have just stated,
because to do so I would need to explore not only Shakespeare's sources and personal experiences but also their temporal relations to other events.[15] I must be content to cite an
example related to our present theme which should show the
trend of spiritual belief over the sexual era and into contemporary psychology. As a point of departure for his *Merchant
of Venice,* Shakespeare adopted Giovanni Fiorentino's novelistic conception of the ancient spiritual motif relative to
man's sexual abstinence on the first night, which had become
woman's responsibility during the sexual era.[16] In the original
legend the Venetian merchant ran into debt financing three
attempts on the part of his adopted son, Gianetto, to win the
clever and beautiful Lady Belmont. On the first night the
Lady drugged Gianetto and stole his belongings. On the first
and second nights she condemned him to involuntary abstinence, which symbolized man's wish under the original
spiritual belief. At Gianetto's third attempt, which meant the
"third night" in spiritual terms, a female servant warned him

---

[15] I hope to do this later in a separate study of Shakespeare.

[16] See Simrock's *Sources of Shakespeare* (Quellen des Shakespeare), Berlin,
1831. The novel depicts the first of four days in the *pecorone,* and is supposedly a creation based on the *Gestis Romanorum.*

of the sleeping potion and enabled him to win his lady, so that in a roundabout way he still exercised spiritual foresight and renounced his sexual resistance only by abstaining as spiritual belief dictated.

If the foregoing illustration represents another "interpretative" projection of man's spiritual anxiety on sexually resistant woman, this motif is entirely lacking in the *Merchant of Venice,* which substitutes for it the novelistic theme of a choice amongst several small boxes or caskets.[17] This latter motif suggests the basic one, only in that the hero left two of the caskets untouched and opened the third. But like the Portia act, this whole episode serves the dramatist only as a foil for his creation of Shylock who, although human, still lacked that spiritual quality which would have made him a definite personification of the Devil. The legal texture of the act makes it a true Devil's pact, though the much criticized sophistical solution of the plot was not a *deus ex machina* but a *diabolus ex machina* in which the Devil was cheated not only of his money but of a Christian soul symbolized by blood. Just as the blasphemous Don Juan was well suited to portray a sexual Devil, the unspiritual Jew was an appropriate representation of a money Devil.

It is interesting that as in Don Juan the success of Shakespeare's humanization of the legend should have remained unrecognized as such. This art of characterization, which presupposes a great personal gift on Shakespeare's part, appeared in an era in which sexual ideology was declining under Christianity's influence and was about to be replaced by a psychological and motivational doctrine of the soul. Accordingly, a further parallel may be drawn between the

[17] See Freud: "The Motif of the Choice of the Casket" (Das Motiv der Kästchenwahl), *Imago,* II, 1913.

Spanish and English dramatists. In *Hamlet* Shakespeare interpreted characterologically another spiritual theme which had played a prominent role in Don Juan and which concerns the victim of murder who finds no rest in his grave. Without any question, it seems to me that the "stone visitor" and the ghost of Hamlet's father were not only similar in appearance but were products of the same fundamental kind of thinking.[18] In *Don Juan* it was Donna Anna who avenged her father's death, because there was no son to carry out the blood revenge. Hamlet was not incapable of executing this task, because he finally did accomplish it; he only delayed the vengeance to which tradition ascribed a mythical motive, and to which Shakespeare gave a psychological motive. Therefore in explaining Hamlet, one never really achieves an understanding of Shakespeare himself, because the latter's account was just a many-sided characterological motivation and psychological interpretation of a long-forgotten spiritual meaning which Freud could not discover even with the help of the Oedipus complex. In depicting the hero as a hesitant and melancholy neurotic type, Shakespeare gives a psychological account of both his theme and the hero. This account depicts, but does not explain, the postponement of the act. Freud accounted for the underlying spiritual motif in terms of an ideology of the sexual era, and consequently had to use the Oedipus myth. Yet what is the basic spiritual content which tradition motivated mythologically as feigned stupidity, which Shakespeare explained characterologically as psychological inhibition, and which psychoanalysis has interpreted as incest wish under a sexual ideology of the soul? This spiritual motif obviously inheres in the ghost of the

---

[18] I have already drawn the parallel in "The Don Juan Character" (Don Juan Gestalt).

murdered person, whose immortality was a persistent curse because his soul was bound to the dead body and could not find a new one. This tie created the duty of blood vengeance which a son was obliged to carry out upon the murderer, but which also consigned the son to the blood avenger of *his* victim. Such a process is the *vendetta,* which often exterminates whole families or clans, and parallels for which may be found in the Greek Tantalid legend, among North American Indians, in the history of the Italian Renaissance, and elsewhere. As a presumptive blood avenger, Hamlet was in constant danger of his life, so that his postponement of his own act of vengeance could not possibly have been motivated by a desire to prolong or save his own life.[18a]

However, this proves to be true in a more personal sense. Legendary motivation of Hamlet's action with the mythical motif of pseudoinsanity, or simulated delusion, gave him a protective disqualification for the task imposed by circumstance, just as Odysseus, to whom Helen meant nothing, had simulated delusions when he took the field with Agamemnon and Menelaus to free her from her abductors. This simulation amounted to a rejection of duty, which will-psychology regards as an *inability* to act.[19] Shakespeare was being psychologically consistent when he let Hamlet manifest pseudoinsanity, because the simulated delusions were almost real. Hamlet ultimately became an inhibited, neurotic type who was unable to do what he had previously not wanted to do. Because of our accent on the basic will-conflict, the problem becomes the purely internal one sensed by Shakespeare, and

---

[18a] See Jos. Kohler: *Shakespeare before the Forum of Jurisprudence* (Shakespeare vor dem Forum der Jurisprudenz), Würzburg, 1894; also *The Principle of Blood Vengeance* (Zur Lehre von der Blutrache), Würzburg, 1885.

[19] See *Truth and Reality* (Wahrheit und Wirklichkeit), 1929.

concerns the reason for Hamlet's not wanting to act rather than for his inability to act. The reason lay in his revolt against his father's control over his soul and life.

In order to appreciate the full ontogenetic significance of this matter, we must think of the change undergone by the problem of immortality during the sexual era. A common legend which I recapitulated in *The Myth of the Birth of the Hero* (Mythus von der Geburt des Helden, 1st ed., 1908; 2nd ed., 1922) shows that during the matriarchal era a father opposed his son in many ways which signified his objection to giving up individual immortality for procreative immortality. Two such customs were infanticide and child exposure, which were foreign to primitive peoples but common to the heroic legends of civilized peoples. In conformity with primitive spiritual thinking, the spiritual resistance which primitive man had to the child as a spiritual heritage was expressed in the unique institution of *couvade,* or "paternal parturiency." In contrast with child exposure of the sexual era, one may recognize in primitive couvade a spiritual reaction on the father's part, which implied his acceptance of the child as the familial bearer of the soul. It was quite logical for the father to become spiritually ill at the time of his child's birth, because the child now received his soul from the father instead of from the collective soul or totem. Relinquishing a part of his soul to the child weakened the father almost to the point of death, and, because of his subsequent recovery, couvade signified a reconciliation between collective spiritual belief and partially accepted fatherhood.

In the sexual era the father, who did not want to be killed or weakened by his son, exposed him not only to counteract the child's threat to his own life but to prolong his own life, as a number of legends will show. The devouring of children

63

by Kronos, the Nordic legend of King Aun,[20] and all like traditions indicate that the father was trying to recover his own soul-material through a kind of incorporation of his son. As Hamlet's duty signifies, this "ingestion" of paternal soul-stuff became just a legal, and finally a "moral," obligation for the son to sacrifice his own life and happiness for his dead father.

In his mythological and psychological refusal to avenge his father, which his simulated insanity and will-inhibition respectively betray, the son tried to destroy his spiritual relationship to his father, just as the father had once tried to disown his own spiritual perpetuation in his son. The son tried not only to emphasize his own individuality, but to win immortality for himself. As the father had done in the sexual era, the son also rejected the idea that he was a son begotten by his father, and reverted to the naïve spiritual belief that he had been conceived spiritually and not sexually. Numerous myths from the sexual era symbolize this primitive spiritual idea by the mother's dreams of conception, which were obvious substitutes for divine impregnation, and were incompatible with the mother's conserving role during this transitional matriarchal period.

Let us return to the son, whose disguise of insanity and denial of sexual knowledge served to liberate him from his father. This pretense implies that Hamlet underwent the sexual test in order to prove his sanity, his recognition of biological descent from his father, and his resultant obligation to execute blood vengeance. In the saga Hamlet knew how

[20] Aun sacrificed nine sons to Odin, and thereby added so many years to his own life that he finally suckled like a child and could not stand without support (Ynglinga saga, chap. 29). My *Incest Motif* (Inzest-Motiv), 2nd ed., page 289, refers to other legends like this one.

PSYCHOLOGY AND THE SEXUAL ERA

to circumvent such tests, for he left the maiden untouched (abstinence) while eavesdroppers were near, and seduced her later in an out-of-the-way place. In the drama which betrays Shakespeare's characteristic rejection of woman, Hamlet both abstained and preached abstinence to his mother, while playing the obscene fool for whom sex was a pleasure devoid of all spiritual significance.

Thus Hamlet's indecisiveness, which Shakespeare worked into a neurotic character study, was just the psychological expression of an ancient spiritual motif currently manifested as a son's unwillingness to accept the duty imposed on him by his father. Instead of sacrificing himself for his father, he used such indecision to emphasize his own individuality in the sense of ancient spiritual belief in immortality because he wanted to save his soul as well as his life. Consequently Shakespearian drama employed a device used with every son-hero in mythology, which made such heroes immune to all kinds of injury until they had completed their life tasks. Heroes acquired such defenses from their mothers both physically (see birth legends) and in the spiritual sense of matriarchy, and it was to their mothers and not to their fathers that they were indebted for their souls and immortality. Moreover, as in the original version of Hamlet, the mother was the son's ally who deceived and consoled the selfish father by exposing a different child. Certain legends in which this substitute child appears as the hero's twin brother depict the twin as the hero's Double or guardian angel who not only protected him but died to save his life. The clearest idea of a dual, or mortal and immortal, soul is to be found among North American Indians who incorporated both individual and supra-individual parts of the soul into the ego or self. And, strange to say, this action connected the idea of a personal guardian soul with the generic totem spirit rather than with the individual body soul.[21] It seems that this connection was made because the corporeal member of the double soul was no longer believed to survive death, as had been the case in the preanimistic era, and because the corporeal soul had been displaced by the totemistic collective soul which was conceived of individually as a personal guardian soul.

In both the saga and drama of Hamlet, this physical inviolacy against all attack is apparent not only in Hamlet's guardian spirit Double, Horatio, but in the fact of Hamlet's death by a poisoned sword, just as though he had been charmed against injury by ordinary weapons. However, unlike his heroic prototype, Hamlet was not just protected up to the fulfillment of his life task, but this very fulfillment itself proved his immortality and transformed him from a son into an individual. His return from the grave proved his capacity to survive tests of the lower world as well. But, unlike the spirit of his father, he returned as a living hero to avenge the threats to his life and happiness (Ophelia). This was Hamlet's turning point, because he could then prove not only the king's murderous intent but its involvement of himself. He was finally able to achieve blood vengeance because he could then act in self-defense and on his own will, instead of in obedience to his father. This developmental step resolves the whole problem of will and fate, and of procreation and individualization. Shakespeare's Hamlet seems to interpret the conflict between the son's procreative life task as receiver and giver

[21] See Levy-Bruhl: *How Natives Think* (Die geistige Welt des Primitiven, München, 1927, p. 100 f); German translation of *Les fonctions mentales dans les sociétés inférieures*. The English version was published by Alfred A. Knopf, New York, in 1926.

of the soul, and his personal life task as guardian of his own immortality in terms of a type psychology characteristic of the "era of the son." It was not so important that the ancient spiritual belief surviving in this material could still be interpreted naturo-mythologically or even sexuo-psychologically, because it was the individual's new attitude that was crucial in this period of the son. The characterological typing signifies a transition from spiritual belief to psychology.

The only meaning of the incest motif inheres in material translated from the mother's spiritual terms into the psychological terms of the son, whose sexual ideology did not outlast patriarchy. For, in the language of the sexual era, the marriage of a murdered father's widow was only an expression of the immortality wish which had been suppressed in nature mythology. As so many scholars[22] have demonstrated, this whole group of sagas rests on a mythical and cultistic treatment of the ancient god of Winter, who suffered death at the hands of Spring, his youthful son, in order that the mother Earth could remarry. But this nature myth itself was only a quasi-scientific attempt to prove human immortality by the analogy of recurrent processes in nature. Its inherent incestuousness again placed sexuality at the service of individual immortality, inasmuch as man was reborn as his own son by his own mother. This theme is suggested by that part of the saga in which Hamlet set out for England and in which he charged his mother to plan a year hence the celebration of his death, to which he would return. Yet when he appeared in the churchyard after his phenomenal rescue at sea, he rose from *Ophelia's* grave.

---

[22] From the Simrock school (See Zinsow: *The Hamlet Saga*, Die Hamletsage, Halle, 1877) to Gilbert Murray: *The Classical Tradition in Poetry*, London, 1927.

In spite of all contrary explanations by legal history and sexual psychology, Shakespeare's Hamlet rejected both the blood vengeance which served paternal immortality[22a] and the incest which symbolized the sexual ideology of immortality. In pre-Shakespearian, Elizabethan drama of the Renaissance, which drew heavily from Seneca's incestuous and blood vengeful prototypes,[23] this inner conflict of the individual was scarcely mentioned. Shakespeare took over this stageworthy motif, but intensified it in relation to his own personal experiences by interpreting the older intellectualized and sexualized material in his psychological character types. In Shakespeare's hands, diabolical Shylock, who was thought to be a stealer of souls, turned out to be a pettifogging lawyer. Hamlet, who was concerned with the welfare of his soul, became a character hesitant and unfaithful to duty. And Gertrude, stripped of her honor of motherhood, became a lascivious wanton. Because of his psychologizing, Shakespeare could not appreciate woman as an ancient spiritual character, but always characterized her as bad. At the beginning of the sexual era woman's veneration as bearer of the soul had granted her the superior status that became hers under matriarchy. In the saga even Helen was not "bad," but her feminine charms inflamed men to fight over her as they would have over the immortal soul which the soul-bearing, maternal woman ultimately represents. Under the influence of the Church and of belief in the Devil, woman became transformed from a symbol of the soul into one of sexuality divorced from the soul. Then

[22a] According to Bachofen's penetrating analysis of the Orestes saga and similar legends, blood vengeance was originally a phase of matriarchy. Like many other phenomena, it sustained paternal power only at a later period.

[23] Without any question, Thyestes' ghost in Seneca's *Agamemnon* seems to be a prototype for the ghost scene in *Hamlet*.

Shakespeare characterized her as evil, as an inferior example of the male sex, and as the seat of far more damnable passions than the male organism could ever possess. Almost all of Shakespeare's female characters were thoroughly bad. We need only to recall Cleopatra, Lady Macbeth, the "Shrew," or Gertrude in order to appreciate Lear's and Timon's hatred for their wives. The sole exception was the daughter, Ophelia. In *The Tempest*, the aging poet who had no sons seemed obliged finally to turn to his daughter. And even though his own unfortunate marriage had certainly contributed to his degradation of woman, it is probably significant that the England of the ascendant Bard was ruled by a powerful woman who was the epitome of feministic dominance as well as of sublime matriarchy.

Hamlet in particular may have represented a reaction of Shakespeare to the death of his father (Brandes) or a painful recollection of his own son, Hamnet, who was long since dead (Freud). Were either possibility true, our conception of the drama as a conflict of spiritual belief would be substantiated. This could be the case even though Hamnet's death belonged to the past, and even though we are ignorant of the date of Shakespeare's first conception of the play, except for the prototypical character of Hamlet, which stemmed ostensibly from Kyd. But all these sources, prototypes, and conceptions lend the material that collective quality which the deeply rooted problem of immortality demands. Hamlet's speculation on immortality, particularly in his first ("to be or not to be") and in his final (churchyard scene) monologue, bears deepest impress of poetic art. In spite of the ghost's return, Hamlet could no longer believe in existence after death (see Seneca's version: "the bourn from which no traveller returns"). But then, like the powerful Renaissance characters of his day (Claudius, Fortinbras), Hamlet could no longer prize earthly existence or abundant living. In the sense of the theme illustrative of this point, Hamlet was able to live without fulfilling his duty of blood vengeance, but he could not die honorably without having fulfilled it. The task was neither too hard for him nor impossible of fulfillment. What he struggled against was the task in itself as something imposed on him from without and not as an expression of someone other than himself. He represented the son-type produced by patriarchy and the sexual era, who was no longer a son, a blood avenger, or a second spouse to his mother, but a freed and autonomous person. This ideology, which veered from the reckless type of Renaissance character to an ethical type, appeared in the concurrent religious thought of the German Reformation, whose major issues concerned immortality (indulgences) and freedom of the will. But what interests us now is just the strictly spiritual ideology which determined reality in all eras, and finally forced the son—the underdog, the proletariat—to assume that attitude which is the ultimate manifestation of individual spiritual belief.

INDIVIDUALISM
AND COLLECTIVISM

> *Two spirits dwell at odds within my breast,*
> *And each would gladly from the other part;*
> *The one seems with the single urge obsessed*
> *To keep the friendly earth within my heart;*
> *The other draws me forth in willful quest*
> *Of visions to a finer world apart.*   GOETHE

THE PRECEDING CHAPTER HAS brought us all the way from religious spiritual belief, through a sexual ideology of immortality, to a humanized portrayal of all these concepts in certain character types and psychological interpretations. This last stage, to which our first chapter referred as projective psychology, was a kind of concretion of spiritual phenomena whose significance had formerly been religious and sexual. Such a personification of spiritual phenomena is extremely ancient, and goes back to the religious era of gods and demons which survived in the Middle Ages as ghosts and devils. The human significance of such entities has remained unrecognized only because they have been viewed from the standpoints of introspective psychology and natural science ideology.

If we bear in mind the evolution which belief in an immortal soul underwent from its inception in preanimistic materialism to our current natural science psychology, we find a certain parallel with the development of chemistry from alchemy, or of astronomy from astrology. But the evolution from spiritual belief to a doctrine of mind was the more radical and fateful development. From their inception, the natural sciences had been humanistic. Babylonian astrology, the metaphysics of the Ionian philosophers, and the alchemy of the black arts of the Middle Ages were all manifestations of spiritual belief: alchemy tried to create the soul artificially (homunculus); and astrology, to read its fate in the stars with which it was identified. The one tried to insure personal immortality by virtue of the soul's connection with the external world soul; the other, by consciously fathoming its secrets. While the natural sciences emerging from primitive spiritual belief tended from the abstract to the concrete and from the spiritual to the practical, spiritual belief originated in a fully conscious and concrete idea of the body's shadow, with the eminently practical purpose of insuring immortality. In scientific psychology such belief became a partly mystical, partly abstract, and certainly incomprehensible concept of the soul. While the natural sciences continued in one way or another to develop the themes of their spiritual prototypes, psychology acquired an antispiritual focus because, unlike the natural sciences, it could neither sustain other forms of belief in the soul nor escape the pressure exerted by its own intellectual analysis to destroy the soul.

If we want to understand this transformation and its significance for man's development, we must begin with an earlier point of view which I have already mentioned. At first, immortality had been thought of in the purely individual sense of survival of the bodily self, but at the stage of spiritual belief it was incorporated into a system properly designated as

72

religious (totemism) which signified a collection or incorporation in the sense of the term *religio*. This unification implied
not a mere collection of various stages of immortality belief
into a religious system, but the incorporation of a number of
individuals under the social dominion of a spiritual system.
We have already suggested that the synthesis of various totem
souls into a generic totem signified a kind of spiritual promiscuity or spiritual communism by which all women of a clan
could satisfy their spiritual needs. This first attempt to sustain
totemistic belief in individual immortality culminated in the
creation of the collective soul, which insured immortality but
transformed the individual survival of the bodily self into
collective survival of the individual spiritual self. In other
words, under the totemistic system, belief in individual immortality was a belief in collective reincarnation based on
socio-spiritual collectivism rather than on reproductive generation. It was not yet a matter of a father who survived in
an individual hereafter, comprised by his own children, but
of souls of the dead incarnated in various animal and plant
spirits, which passed them on to the next generation of the
totem-symbolized clan. This collective soul which found concrete expression in socio-familial unity was a reciprocal guarantee of immortality which always insured the individual's
survival in the next generation. This mutual security of all
family group members in collective immortality was responsible for the powerful and rigid social units of the presexual era,
in which the individual gave up his naïve belief in physical
immortality for an ideology of the family group. It is my
opinion that this ideology offers a basis for understanding
both the bitter hatreds and feuds between North American
Indian tribes, and the feuds or vendettas currently practiced
in many European countries. Whether it was the theft of

73

women under exogamy, or the murder of male members of the tribe, it was always a matter of avenging serious offenses upon the spiritual economy of the community which, being robbed of one of its symbols of spiritual revenue, sought to cancel or at least avenge the shortages created in the immortality account. In contrast with the large civil groupings of the sexual era, which were themselves composed of familial elements, the small group unit such as the tribe or clan was characteristic of animistic, social collectivism. The fact that the individual members of small spiritual groups all knew one another reflects the original materialistic body-soul which became universalized and spiritualized only in Christianity's time. Christianity revived the tribally circumscribed spiritual collectivism within the more inclusive civil organizations of the sexual era in which the concept of the soul was transformed from that of the dead to that of the living (son).

Social organization originally involved not a restriction of the individual, but a protection and extension of his ego through spiritual belief. Natural binding forces for society were fashioned from this communal ego interest. Tabus were not external prohibitions, but tributes which the individual willingly paid, not so much for the common good as for his self-protection which rested on that good. Morals and law were still embodied in community interest which was in effect a collectivized self-interest. The factors inherent in the original tribal units came to serve the new ideology only through an acceptance of the individual's survival in his own children, which characterized the sexual era. By granting him the right to possess his wife and child, and by obliging him not to threaten the spiritual economy of others in the family group, society gave the individual a legal and moral assurance of the immortality embodied in his offspring. In other words, in the

74

sexual era which culminated in familial social structure, that *unity* of the individual with the group, which was founded on spiritual communality and guaranteed the individual's spiritual well-being, was legalized as procreative immortality and moralized as bounden duty. However, both of these ideologies stood in direct opposition to primitive spiritual communality in which the sharing of collective immortality was a self-evident principle, and in which a struggle for individual immortality was a threat to the tribe (tabu).

The transformation of collective spiritual belief into individual familial organization came about gradually and under difficulties of the most diverse kind. We have already described matriarchy as a decisive turning point, and as the first realistic and worldly social manifestation of sexual belief in procreative immortality. While all women had previously belonged to the generic totem or collective soul, and all children to the tribe, under matriarchy the child was awarded to the mother, so that the father remained officially excluded from individual immortality. The same spiritual insecurity which had produced the collective immortality structure of the totem clan prevented man of the sexual era from entirely relinquishing his collective principle for an individual one. He only came to accept his father role spiritually under a *state* which actually had nothing to do with his spiritual significance, and had divorced itself from religion in order to emphasize its legal and moral significance. As the Roman state amply illustrates, man had a guarantee of his procreative immortality under patriarchy, because his children, and his wife, whom he addressed as "dear soul" (*dulcis anima*), were his virtual slaves. Yet, while the state could protect such rights, as a collective agent it could only protect his *soul* legally and morally, and not religiously.

To be sure, the community itself underwent a marked change, from its original denial of a fatherhood which guaranteed collective immortality, to its legal establishment of a fatherhood which guaranteed individual immortality. From a spiritual community which was a *religio* in the strict sense of that word, society was transformed into a legal community with an alienated state religion. This new type of community which included both legal and moral institutions, but in which state and religion coexisted independently, still maintained the illusion of the original collective soul, while the power of the state served a procreative immortality guaranteed by the family rather than by the community. Thus man's familial immortality which had survived from matriarchy was honored only under the state's protection, because the state not only supported the laws governing marriage, but symbolized that collective immortality which had predated marriage itself. The state, which had originally been created to protect the family, gradually undermined and ruined it, for the family had been founded on the individual principle of procreative immortality guaranteed by laws of marriage and succession, while the state and its official religion were the remnants of the immortality principle which the state legalized and religion moralized. These respective actions account for the balanced and common interest of the state and religion in the institution of marriage, which guaranteed collective immortality by religious sanction of the individual, and sexual-individual immortality by his civil sanction.

In this conflict between family and state, which was essentially a conflict between the individual immortality provided by the child and the collective immortality guaranteed by society—or between the religious and sexual eras—the Jews have been the most effectively evasive of all peoples. With their unusual adaptability they have accommodated themselves best to a sexual ideology, sacrificed state for family, and, by "multiplying like the sands of the sea," maintained themselves while other peoples suffered from hypertrophy of statehood. The state has given only partial protection to familial immortality, since in other respects it has remained the representative of the older, collective immortality. And the state has even become a less true representative in this latter sense, because it has always demanded that the individual sacrifice for its maintenance. In contrast, the Jewish state was represented by a religion oriented entirely to worldly affairs, which had no traffic with the hereafter, and placed familial immortality above everything else.[1] It was quite logical, then, for Christianity to mark the Jew as an individualist perpetually damned to a worldly existence ("the eternal Jew").

For Christianity represented an attempt of a different kind, to use religion to preserve the socio-spiritual community of the clan, which the aspiritual kings of the constitutional state had undermined. While Judaism held fast to the reality of world tribal organization, and perpetuated it sexually through the family, Christianity concerned itself with the immortal soul, which it could sustain only in a future state free of humanized qualities. In this sense Judaism and Christianity cannot be compared either historically or religiously. They are simply extreme developments of present- and future-oriented aspects of spiritual belief, which are anchored in social organization and are inseparably united in totemism by the ideology of collective rebirth of the soul. Israel prob-

---

[1] In his *History of Israel* (Geschichte Israels), Renan has brought the anomalous position of the Jews into relation to their attitudes toward the present, and to their lack of an ideology of the hereafter.

ably grew torpid and lost its statehood under a religious and familial ideology of sexual immortality mediated by the family, while Christianity began with a spiritual ideology of immortality in a future state and became at one time a far-flung, realistic world sovereignty to which all nominal rulers of the people voluntarily submitted.

Let us now turn from this spiritual basis of human socialization and its civil and religious forms, to the individual by and for whom all these ideologies and institutions were created. The spiritual collectivism embodied in totemism passed over into a collective socialism rather like that depicted in Plato's ideal state. Women and children represented the collective soul comprised by the clan and its totem. The rise of the sexual era, and its acceptance of the individual's procreative immortality, destroyed this worldly communism which had mirrored spiritual communism. Under matriarchy it was even more definitely an incarnate collective soul which found expression in the role of the mother deity, or Mother Earth, who nourishes and gives life to all, and finally became victorious in the fatherhood and patriarchy of temporal individualism. However, this development required a double guarantee of immortality from the state and civil community: first, a spiritual-collective guarantee through the social phenomena of society and religion; and secondly, an individual-sexual guarantee concretely expressed through such institutions as marriage, the family, and succession by inheritance. This social father-individualism, which tried to relate itself both to the temporal world and to an already uncertain belief in the hereafter, was completely overthrown by Christianity. In its place the son (the individual) and not the father, became the real heir. The role of spiritual bearer of the soul passed from mother to son, whom the sexual era had elevated to the most important position of all, since it was the son who received his father's soul from his mother and passed on his soul to his own son. This accounts for the crucial importance of the son ever since the rise of Christianity, which comprised the transition from the sexual era to that of the child, under whose psychological sign we still find ourselves.

Although the principle of the individual, or son, strongly resisted domination by the father principle at the height of the sexual era, it remained for Christianity to support this principle and to make it completely victorious. For in making the son a bearer of the soul instead of a mere extension of his father's life, Christianity made it possible for him to cease resisting and to accept his role as son. In the heroic myths of antiquity the son had to carry out certain tasks in order to vindicate his earthly existence, but Christianity could now grant him immortality without imposing such tasks. The soul had found collective and social symbolizations in matriarchy and the father concept; the Christian concept of the son gave it its first *individual* incarnation. At the same time, Christianity encompassed both of the other spiritual concepts in its synthesis of the Trinity and lifted totemistic belief in transmigration beyond the stage of paternal, procreative immortality into an individual, spiritual role of the son. Thus the collective spiritual role of woman as mother and the sexual individualism of the father were harmonized in an individual spiritual role of the son. On the other hand, as he matured into fatherhood, the son became the seat of conflict and, to his own children, the giver of those recently contending spiritual and sexual ideologies which he represented.

Thus, with the support of Christianity, the spiritual individualism of the son precipitated new trends, ideologies, and conflicts, which the individual was obliged somehow to

79

resolve. He now had to create what society could no longer offer him because he was no longer a mere member of society, but an independent entity, or microcosm, who opposed society and the world. Before we pursue the interesting expression of spiritual individualism in scientific psychology as a doctrine of the soul, let us epitomize this entire development in another literary symbol. Just as we found sexual individualism in Don Juan, and psychological neurotic individualism in Shakespeare's Hamlet, we may now discover spiritual individualism in Goethe's Faust.

Faust initially tried to win immortality with the help of alchemy and astrology, the secret "black art" sciences of his era, and with the legitimate sciences of Goethe's era; but he became a captive of the Devil, to whom he had already paid his own life. This pact with the Devil symbolized the individual's attempt to insure the mastery of his own soul by renouncing collective, spiritual community for the sake of his immediate pleasure. Here are the "two souls in the human breast," the mortal and the immortal, the individual and the collective, the one exemplified in the totemistic North American Indians' physical vitality for earthly living (*mana*), and the other by the immortal guardian spirit incarnate or the noble soul.[1a] The Devil was the guardian spirit, or collective, immortal soul, transformed into an incarnation of the individual, temporal, or mortal soul, so that it was only logical for him to have promised long life in return for the immortal soul, and sensual satisfaction for sexual immortality. The idealized image of Helen represented the immortal soul of the sexual era personified in woman whom Faust pursued like a will-o'-

---

[1a] Just as Plato dealt with two conflicting halves of the soul, the doctrine of Mani (300 A.D.) was concerned with two perpetually conflicting souls which poets had mentioned prior to Goethe's time (Racine, Wieland).

the-wisp. In the end, and in a way typical of the era of the son, Faust achieved immortality in his own acts and works, and so rededicated himself to humanity.

We can now begin to understand man's role as an individual creator of culture, in which he was obliged both to overcome spiritual collective immortality and sexual procreative immortality, and to discover new symbols, forms, and means of expression for the many different manifestations of his own individuality and of individualism in general. True to her original role of bearer of the collective soul, woman remained a symbol of the principle of conservation, while man assumed the role of the transitory, mortal soul which could survive only in ever-changing symbols. This spiritual inferiority of man relative to woman might appear to be a product of the sexual era whose spiritual and social groundwork had been prepared by matriarchy, but it was essentially a biological and social inferiority in the sense of procreative immortality. To console his ego, man looked upon this inferiority as though it were only psychological, and tried to dissociate himself from it as much as he could. While such dissociation was to his advantage under an animistic belief in individual immortality, it was a liability under collectivistic spiritual belief, so that he suffered inferiority again under the sexual ideology of procreative immortality. In contrast, woman rose from a mere agent of spiritual fructification and rebirth to become the creative bearer of the soul and the agent of mortality and immortality. And although man's original ideology of immortality rested on a complete denial of woman, he became completely bound to her in order to proclaim his individual independence through the self-immortalization inherent in his works.

All these tendencies culminate in Romanticism, which concerns a unique attitude toward the soul and its individualized forms. Two aspects of Romanticism significant for the development of psychology are romantic love which reëvaluated woman spiritually in relation to individualism, and romantic science which did homage to such collectivistic productions as ballads, epics, myths, and fairy tales, and revived the concept of the cosmic nature-soul. Romantic love led to sexual psychology,[2] while romantic science led to natural philosophy and anthropological psychology.[3] In combination with poetic characterology, sense physiology, and experimental psychology, both of these developments led to our present psychological era; but they are understandable only in relation to the spiritual significance of Romanticism, which brought the ancient concept of the soul to the fore under the ideology of the individualistic era of the son. This was the concept embodied in the collective soul of the animistic era, and in the mother-soul of the sexual era. In Romanticism, woman as an individual represented the immortal soul principle in man, which she had represented collectively under the matriarchy of the spiritual era, and imaginatively in the mythical traditions of the sexual era (Helen, Psyche, and fairy tales). In romantic love, she was man's better, eternal, and "beautiful soul"[4] to which his transitory and creative individual ego[5]

[2] See especially Wilhelm von Humboldt: *Sexual Differences* (Ueber den Geschlechtsunterschied), 1795, new edition by Giese, Langensalza, 1917. More recent studies: F. Giese: *The Romantic Character. I. The Evolution of the Problem of Androgyny in Early Romanticism.* (Der Romantische Charakter. I. Die Entwicklung der Androgynenproblems in der Frühromantik), Langensalza, 1919. Also Klucksohn: *The Romantic Concept of Love* (Die Auffassung der Liebe in der Romantik), Halle, 1922.

[3] See Karl Joël: *Origin of Natural Philosophy in the Spirit of Mysticism* (Der Ursprung der Naturphilosophie aus dem Geiste der Mystik), Jena, 1906.

[4] Plato mentions the "beautiful soul" in his Symposium, whose romantic conception by Wieland had its precursors in Shaftesbury, the English moral

82

was opposed. Woman's idealization was a reaction against her moralization by Christian ideology, which had identified her with sexuality and damned her as a witch, and against the resultant psychologizing (Shakespeare) which characterized her as "evil." Romanticism lifted these moral and psychological evaluations into a sphere of feeling in which the individual ego lost its identity, just as the individual had once been part of a generic world-soul which romantic science now transformed into a "Nature soul."

In this partly poetic, partly philosophical tendency of the romantic ego to immortalize itself, feelings became objects of psychology. As such they were not mere ego expressions, but still bore that pervasive meaning given them by Goethe, who asserted that "Feeling is everything." This development engendered the romantic interest in folk psychology and in the creations of entire peoples which the collective soul used to counteract romantic individualism. The romantic problem of the true origins of such collective and anonymous works as myths, fables, epics, and ballads seems to me to be just a psychologizing attitude in the face of the fact that such works *treated* of peoples and of their destinies. This last fact is important, whether the treatment was direct, as in the historical epic which depicted a people's ephemerality and immortalized its accomplishments in man's memory; or whether it was indirect, as in the spiritual myth of a hero who symbolized the people, or of gods who were immortalizations of

philosopher, and in the poet Richardson, who gave the concept a moral coloring. Compare also Schiller's definition, which involves a complete agreement between moral sense and sensory affect: *Grace and Virtue* (Anmut und Würde), 1793.

[5] See Hugo Horwitz: *The Ego Problem of Romanticism. The Position of Friedrich von Schlegel in Modern Cultural History* (Das Ich-Problem der Romantik. Die hist. Stellung Fr. Schlegels innerhalb der modernen Geistesgeschichte), München, 1916.

the hero. In the psychological question whether these spiritual creations about heroes, peoples, and gods were the work of individuals or peoples, we encounter the old problem of the relation of the individual to the group, as it is expressed in the related problems of Christ's historical authenticity and the soul's existence. Thus folk psychology again tried to involve the concept of the collective soul,[6] while the characterological psychology of the poets who followed Shakespeare individualized spiritual symbols which portrayed the good immortal soul and bad mortal soul (angel and devil) as good and bad characters instead of as gods and heroes.

Thus, up to the nineteenth century when it emerged as a natural science, psychology really represented the soul and various aspects of spiritual belief. Knowledge of the soul, which religious dogma had regarded as unattainable by man, was definitely not of psychological concern. The existence of the soul, which involves the question of belief in immortality, was either assumed or denied, the one or the other alternative being as undemonstrable as the existence or nonexistence of God. The real threat to the soul lay not with the atheistic natural scientists, but with the individualistic soul-seekers who felt that they had to win their immortality independently of collectivistic spiritual ideology and beyond procreative sexual ideology, and whose need for personal immortality could be satisfied neither by the family or religion, nor by the state or people, which stood for both.

The real danger lay in the psychology of the individual, which had grown out of an increasing knowledge of conscious processes and the self, and had first appeared in Greece in opposition to Plato, the soul's great advocate. Because of

[6] See Friedrich Schlegel: *The Soul* (Von der Seele), 1823 (with an introduction by Günther Müller), Augsburg, 1927.

his natural science orientation, Plato's pupil and successor, Aristotle, was the first to reclaim the soul as an object of research by methods outlined in his Organon.[7] Aristotle's psychology, or soul doctrine, belonged methodologically to physics. He subsumed spiritual materials under an ethics based on free will and under a metaphysics concerned with the concept of an impalpable God. Therefore, in preserving the soul ethically in terms of freedom of will and metaphysically in terms of God, he achieved the first natural scientific psychology. After a pervasive Christian theology had disclosed this first scientific attempt to concretize the soul, philosophers of the Middle Ages and of more recent times were lured into the same detour.

In the first chapter of the present volume we have already outlined the history of psychology, which became a science only by the nineteenth century.[7a] We should like then to consider the role which individual self-awareness played in the evolution of psychology from the spiritual era to the professedly exact science of psychoanalysis.

In this connection it must be said that Christianity, which had survived all inner doubts and had triumphed over all attempts to alienate it from ancient spiritual belief, finally found an externalized opponent in science. But knowledge of philosophy and natural science could find as little with which to incriminate spiritual belief in immortality as knowledge of natural life processes had found to oppose man's naïve belief

---

[7] See Aristotle's *Minor Natural Science Writings* (Parva Naturalia) (Kleine naturwissensch. Schriften), edited by von Rolfes, Leipzig, 1924 (Philos. Bibl., vol. 6). Also: Werner Jäger's *Aristotle. Introduction to a History of his Development* (Aristoteles. Grundlegung einer Geschichte seiner Entwicklung), Berlin, 1923.

[7a] See Friedrich Seifert's excellent presentation in his *Handbuch der Philosophie:* "Psychology, metaphysics of the soul" (Psychologie, Metaphysik der Seele), München, 1928.

in immortality. As is well known, science owed its greatest advances to the thinkers and investigators who were believers in a deep, spiritual sense of the word. Belief and knowledge are interdependent, and not mutually exclusive; it is rather self-awareness that inevitably leads to *doubt*. Knowledge of death had been unable to shake belief in individual immortality. Yet the intellectual curiosity to understand and to conceptualize, to see a thing as completely as possible, to explain, to comprehend, and to demonstrate, all produced the greatest doubt in the individual, particularly regarding the existence of his soul.

Just as the conflict between temporal and external beliefs and values ruled the Middle Ages, that between religion and science characterizes modern times. Until now the Church has been the victor in all these struggles because it offered the individual something which science both denied and lacked. All these bitter conflicts are really centered on one question: Is the individual immortal, and, therefore, is there a soul? Fleeting, worldly existence was less at stake than was the eternal bliss that religion promised, science denied, and psychological knowledge doubted. It is from this doubt that we suffer, and not from knowledge against which one can set belief, for belief cannot prevail against doubt. So man has tried to set up a new God to combat the Devil, a deity born of ancient spiritual belief but fathered by scientific intellectualism. This new god was Truth.

Since progressive self-awareness had undermined belief in the soul, self-knowledge, which was the unwonted by-product of the growth of individualism, became all important, so that the necessity of tormenting self-awareness became the virtue of therapeutic self-knowledge, whose results were esteemed as "truth." However, since our intellectual processes are tied in with our wishes and passions and are determined by them, truth became a subjective or intellectualized individual religion which could be used to sustain man's ancient spiritual beliefs. And, in place of knowledge under collective belief (what *everyone* believes constitutes truth), individualism says, "What *I* believe is true." Religion's "I believe, therefore I am" (immortal) developed from philosophy's "I doubt, therefore I am" (aware of myself and therefore mortal) into Cartesian psychology's "I think, therefore I am." With the help of psychology the ego tried thereafter to define its own truth. This was a final intellectual attempt to rescue the soul, but one which actually concealed the soul so cleverly behind an abstract concept of truth that it took all the forces of symbolism to incorporate the old spiritual belief into a cult of truth. Truth, which one cannot gaze upon and live, is the soul. Oddly enough, both entities are often symbolized by a naked woman. Every conflict over truth is in the last analysis just the same old struggle over the existence and immortality of the soul. The spiritual belief that was almost annihilated by psychological self-knowledge was reborn as truth, the supreme idol of psychology. In fact, spiritual belief became a kind of criterion of truth, because only general and therefore everlasting truth could be used to prove belief in immortality.

We encounter this phenomenon even in the case of psychoanalysis, whose effect upon man stems from the animistic attitude shown in its respect for dreams, the unconscious, and the mystery of sex, and not from the individualistic aspects of its knowledge of the self and the soul. Psychoanalysis is psychological knowledge only to a minor degree; it is principally an interpretation of old animistic spiritual

87

values into the scientific language of the sexual era. Even under this sexuo-psychological interpretation, spiritual values are just as comforting or "therapeutic" for us as a naïve belief in immortality was for primitive man. However, Freud consistently[8] renounced this deeper, esoteric content of psychoanalysis in favor of a natural science ideology that regarded the individual statically, and not as an entity which continuously develops through self-creation. Yet these spiritual values which psychoanalysis renounced in the interest of an ideology of truth are effective in their own right, for they have not only advanced man's knowledge of the soul, but have strengthened his belief in it. One can understand why psychoanalysis is praised by poets as antimaterialistic, condemned by philosophers as hyperrationalistic, and damned by religious authorities as materialistic. Psychoanalysis offers no new world view. It is only an attempt to reinterpret an old one, and a confused system which needs psychological analysis in order to make it meaningful. I believe that, in the sense of my explanation, psychoanalysis accounts for the tendency to interpret spiritual phenomena psychologically under a sexual ideology.

The character of psychoanalysis as a psychological savior of the soul is best depicted by its two quite different offshoots: Jung's collective psychology and Adler's individual psychology. Each of these theories develops unilaterally only one of the otherwise integrated aspects of psychoanalytic doctrine, and neglects Freud's characteristic natural science ideology of sex. For Adler, with whom the rational methods

[8] See: *Human Problems in Freudian Psychoanalysis. Original and Mask. A Study of Modern Mental Science.* (Die Menschheitsproblematik der Freudschen Psychoanalyse. Urbild und Maske. Eine grundsätzliche Untersuchung zur neueren Seelenforschung) by E. Michaelis, Leipzig, 1925.

of psychoanalytic interpretation became hypertrophied, there remains absolutely no unconscious or soul. Jung's collective unconscious stands much closer to the soul than did Freud's individualistically conceived unconscious, which remained individualistic even when formulated as the "Id." If Adler's individual psychology was too rational in the sense of conscious interpretation of the ego, Jung's collective psychology was too irrational. The former was too psychological; the latter, too religious, as Freud's doctrine was too biological. Freud made collectivity rational because he sexualized it by interpreting it in terms of procreative sexual ideology. Jung, again, explained individual psychological matters collectively by using the ancient concept of the soul as a basis for psychological explanation, but he merely portrayed a spiritual phenomenon. Adler, who rationalized everything spiritual according to individual psychology, found collectivity in society, just as Jung found it in religion, and Freud, in biology. While Freud treated sexual facts ideologically, Jung made a psychological fact out of collective spiritual ideology, and Adler derived an individualistic ideology from social fact.

One cannot deny that each of these authors covers all sides of the total problem to a certain extent, but, in his ambition to find the psychological explanation of phenomena, each fails to study the varying and peculiar values involved, including that of explanation itself, which is only an interpretation of phenomena. Facts are no more explained by reëvaluating them ideologically than ideologies are explained by labeling them as psychological facts. The materials of psychology are not facts, but ideologies, such as spiritual beliefs, which again are not simply facts related to a definite reality, but ideologies related to a definite mentality. Such concrete manifestations of these ideologies as society or the family must be understood for what they are and not as mere psychological facts.

The soul, which is itself an ideology derived from belief in immortality, continually creates new ideologies which serve only to sustain spiritual belief. However, in making these ideologies the object of introspective awareness, psychology destroys them, because it replaces them with others which lose their value as individualistic self-awareness expands. Yet, as is evidenced by the increasing socialization of phenomena that were once spiritual in the collective sense, these ideologies tend toward greater concreteness in an effort to protect themselves from the impact of introspective consciousness. And, on the other hand, we witness the emotionalization of such collectively spiritual phenomena as morality, which becomes expressed not only as a social fear of punishment but as a subjective feeling of guilt. Just as society first symbolized the salvation and the guarantee of an individual's spiritual immortality, the moral feelings of all of us echo this spiritual communality which inwardly resists our individual struggle for immortality, be such immortality a primitive perpetuation of our personal selves in works, or a sensual sexuality wholly devoid of procreative character. The conflict between morality and sexuality, which is not something imposed on the individual from without but arises from within to protect his integrity, corresponds again to the conflict between individualism and collectivism. For the individual wish for immortality is basically egoistic and antisexual; and, as an expression of collective belief in immortality, the sexual morality in which this wish is inwardly manifested is just as strong as, if not stronger than, the procreative immortality which the sex drive makes possible. In his moral reactions of fear and guilt, man preserves the individuality inherent in his spiritual self-survival, just as society had helped him keep his individuality and his soul by granting him collective immortality.

This conception of morality as a social salvation of the individual and as a representative of the collective soul explains the punishing role which society must assume against the criminal. Murder is a crime against society, which it robs of a soul by destroying an individual who contributes a soul to it. The original *jus talionis*, or "soul for a soul," was transmitted from generation to generation even before society charged the next male descendant with the responsibility for blood vengeance. Society opposed murder as the theft of a soul because it regarded the killing of any soul-bearer as a crime against itself. This created the strictly legal paradox that society punishes a murderer by committing his own crime against him, and actually expiates the theft of a soul by blood vengeance upon the substitute soul *(talion)*. Thus group psychology actually concerns only the soul which is composed of the separate souls of individuals, while individual psychology now tries again both to demonstrate the reality of man's individual soul scientifically and to rescue it from collective ideology with the help of an individual mortality.

A concretion and emotionalization, such as the collective soul experienced in social and moral settings, finally brought the individual soul of the sexual era to the experience of love, in which the immortal spiritual part of the individual became personified in another person, the beloved. Late Christian Romanticism only actualized this ideology, since the pre-Christian, sexual era had already introduced the spiritualization of sexuality which the Church tabued. Romantic love was a significant compromise between individual and collective spiritual demands, because it represented a "collectivity of two." But after a time even this attempted solution proved untenable, and it collapsed before the resurgence of individualism which resisted such an extreme absorption of one individual by another. A person no longer wanted to be used as another's soul even with its attendant compensations. The trouble was that it also menaced one's individuality and restricted one's personal development and desires. The reaction to this conflict inherent in romantic love is expressed by the modern overemphasis on the bodily self and purely sensual matters, and by the current despiritualization of love.

We have now surveyed the stages of spiritual development, from physical individualism of the shadow-soul, through spiritual collectivism of the divine soul and the physical collectivism of sexual procreation, to the spiritual individualism of love which strives for the harmonious unification of all factors. The neurotic is an individual incapable of love because he has lost spiritual (religious) and physical (sexual) collectivity in his attempt to regress from an individual spiritual belief provided by love to a primitive belief in himself, without the help of the naïveté necessary to such self-acceptance. The neurotic loses every kind of collective spirituality, and makes a heroic gesture of placing himself entirely within the immortality of his own ego, as the observations and cosmic fantasies of psychotics so clearly show. The content of such fantasies is mythical and religious because it represents essentially an attempt to salvage belief in the soul with the help of religious and sexual ideologies. As such, it is just like the individual's attempt to transcend

92

these ideologies. Neuroses not only portray this conflict between individual and collective immortality, but depict the ego's attempt to resolve both of these counterparts of the mortal and immortal aspects of spirituality in animistic, social, or sexual terms. One final characteristic of neurotics is of paramount importance. They not only strive for an individual religion (immortality), but they also represent *par excellence* that type of individual whose agonizing self-awareness destroys his own apotheosis, and who gains for his efforts toward creative, spiritual self-realization only a destructive interpretation of his soul.

DREAM
AND REALITY

> *We are such stuff*
> *As dreams are made on, and our little life*
> *Is rounded with a sleep.* SHAKESPEARE

THE PRECEDING CHAPTER SURVEYED
the religious, sexual, and psychological stages of spiritual history. The present one concerns the dream, which is not only a spiritual phenomenon *par excellence*, but also the most subjective and mystical of all mental phenomena, and a phenomenon more inclusive than the dreamer himself, because it allows him both to observe himself and to be at one with the universe.

Man has long been intrigued by such phenomena, but he has not really learned much worth knowing about dreams *as such* because of his greater concern with what they *mean*, if anything. Primitive man believed that dreams had a special, divine significance; and whether they were responsible for animism, or *vice versa*, animistic man regarded them as evidence of his soul and its immortality. These two affirmative beliefs, on the one hand, and modern science's anti-spiritual denial that dreams are meaningful, on the other, serve to show how attitudes toward spiritual belief have variously conditioned the interpretation of dreams from time to time.

94

On this basis one may understand how primitive man could accept dreams of dead persons or his Double as evidence of his soul, and why during the sexual era man's "dreams of conception" and of unborn souls had a religious significance at odds with their erotic meaning. In certain totemistic Australian tribes, conception by the spirit's Double was announced to a mother or father in dreams that disclosed the name, the totem, and even the sex of the child.[1] In the sexual era these dreams signified an ideology of procreative immortality, because then a husband or father who feared death at the hands of his forebears or descendants had anxiety dreams of their departed or unborn souls. At this time a woman's dreams also involved the idea of divine conception, by which her husband sought to preserve his old spiritual beliefs. After supplanting sexual ideology, Christianity regarded this kind of reassurance as wanton, and psychology finally called it a simple wish fulfillment of sexual libido.

Setting aside for the moment a discussion of psychoanalysis, which stresses the dream but denies the soul, let us again consider the naïve concept of the soul. In general, not only were dreams interpreted in terms of a currently ruling ideology, but in creating certain religious and social forms this ideology also evoked certain dream forms and experiences. The dreams were then fitted the more promptly into the current ideology, the closer both the dream and the ideology still stood to their common origin in spiritual belief. In the primitive era of animism and magic, dream and reality coincided completely, because they were both undisguised

---

[1] See the excellent section on "The meaning of dreams" (Bedeutung des Traumes) in Karl Beth: *Religion and Magic* (Religion und Magie), second edition, 1927.

expressions of the spiritual world view. Primitive man therefore failed to interpret dreams, not because interpretation was beyond him, but because his point of view made interpretation unnecessary. He felt this way because of his thorough adherence to the spiritual world view, which made his dream life more basic than his waking reality. And since the soul that was disclosed to the dreamer was unhampered by external circumstances, *primitive man interpreted reality in terms of his dreams,* and in so doing demonstrated a remarkable faculty for discovering their significance. When reality did not correspond to a dream, man simply corrected, influenced, and changed reality to fit the dream's spiritual meaning.

Certain North American Indian tribes who have been observed and described by French Jesuit missionaries[2] felt compelled to carry out their dreams in real life, because otherwise the guardian spirit of the dream would be offended and the dreamer would die.

> The dream is the oracle which all these people question and follow, the prophet who predicts things to come, the Cassandra who proclaims threatening misfortunes, the common physician for all ailments . . . it is their absolute ruler . . . it is their Mercury in their travels, their economy in the family; the dream often guides their assemblies; trading, fishing, hunting are customarily taken with its consent and seem almost to exist in order to conform to it; there is nothing, be it ever so costly, which they would not deny themselves for the sake of a dream. . . . It is actually the Huron's chief deity.[3]

[2] Cited from Levy-Brühl: *How Natives Think* (Die geistige Welt der Primitiven), Munich, 1927, p. 94 ff.
[3] *Communication by the Jesuits* (Relation des Jesuites), X, 1636, p. 170.

Another Father[4] relates that

> In a real sense the Iroquois have only one deity which
> is the dream; they submit to it and follow all its com-
> mands to the letter. The Tsonnontou are even more
> bound to it than are the others; their faith in it is un-
> qualified. What they believe they have done in a dream,
> they feel utterly obliged to carry out as soon as possible.

Similar views, and many examples from South Africa and
Asia Minor such as Levy-Brühl has presented (*loc. cit.*, p.
97), only reinforce the impression that primitive "interpretation" of the dream aims to actualize it and hence to interpret
reality in terms of it.

This interesting fact cannot be *explained* by wish fulfillment, because many of these dreams and their resulting
actions are so obviously concerned directly with wishes and
their fulfillment. Later on we shall see how well will-
psychology explains the transformation of dream into action,
but let us first consider a few consequences of such action.
The view that the individual will die if his dream is not
acted out is explained by Levy-Brühl in terms of an affront
to the guardian spirit (jinni) whose will the dream expressed
(p. 101). But this guardian spirit had closer ties with the
immortal group soul than with the transitory individual soul,
so that this stage portrays the conflict between the individual
and collective souls, which dreams manifested as the mortal
and immortal parts of man, and which often made the fate
of the individual depend upon society's help, and the life
of the community on the individual's willingness to sacrifice
for it. The individual died when his own wish was not

[4] *Ibid.*, LIV, 1669-70, p. 96.

fulfilled, just as when he failed to accede to the wishes of others. While the dream seems here to be an *egoistic* expression of the individual soul and a moralistic expression of the collective soul, this conflict was resolved by the individual's action, which had somehow to meet the needs of the ego as well as the demands of others.

For the present, however, we are interested neither in the psychological motive behind the compulsion to translate dreams into action nor in its psychological consequences for the social behavior of the individual, but in the extent to which this "dream action" survived under the altered relationships of other eras and ideologies. In order not merely to answer this question but also to understand the raising of it, we should focus on the dream's place in the total world picture instead of on its origin and meaning. It is not a question of the possibility or nature of an interpretation but of whether the dream was accepted as true or as a mere phantom of the senses. Primitive man took the dream to be absolutely true, which meant not that he confused it with reality, but that he saw it as a higher reality. The dream neither predicted reality to come nor recalled that which had gone, but portrayed the true reality corresponding to the spiritual world view. This conception of the dream emanated from pure, pre-animistic spiritual belief in the body-soul, according to which the corporeal self endured forever. Since the dream portrayed self-like, corporeal souls of the dead, of the living, and of one's own self, it seemed at first to be confirmed by primal spiritual belief. On this basis the spiritual significance of the dream as proof of the body-soul lay close to a reality whose characters simply seemed to continue acting in the dream experience, so that the phenomenon of the dream itself, apart from its content, proved the existence and independent survival of the bodily soul, not only in the future to which the significance of the dream was subsequently restricted, but literally beyond time and space. The dream's content became important only when it conflicted with waking reality, which in an animistic age was not really violated any more by the appearance of unborn or dead persons in dreams than by the wandering of one's own Double in the upper or lower worlds. To the extent that the dream contradicted reality, the contradiction was neutralized by adjusting reality to suit the dream. The basis for this correction did not lie in any wish merely to improve reality, because this was rarely desired and less often achieved. It lay rather in the compulsion to bring reality into agreement with spiritual belief in order to sustain that belief.

The same tendency to effect a complete agreement between dream and reality throws light on another phenomenon which has won an even more important place in human history than the primitive, spiritual translation of dream into reality. I refer to the telling of the dream as though it were an actual event experienced in the past by one's forebears, or in the present by one's contemporaries. Out of such stories grew myths, fairy tales, and historical fables, which not only worked over the same spiritual motifs as the dream, but corresponded to obviously dreamed events or to accounts of dreams as altered by subsequent action. While such narratives were told even by primitive animistic man, their development into true heroic myths belongs to the sexual era and to its more civilized peoples, the influence of whose ideology appears in the old dream action revised according to the new reality and its conscious content.

The current tendency to actualize dream experiences as such originated with primitives. According to actual statements of North American Indians, dreams comprised their sole source of mythology[5] and prevailed in many of their narratives. Yet even when these tales only report events corresponding to spiritual beliefs, they still sound like dreams because their world view rests on the same ideology from which dreams arose. On this basis it is difficult to determine the extent to which actual events contributed to these verbal accounts; primitive man had to translate his dreams into action, so that his account may refer as well to the one as to the other. For the most part, both dream and action were unintentionally confused by the tendency to make them agree, so that one finds mythical themes only when it is apparent that the dream could not be carried over into reality. The tendency to relate the dream as an actual experience is explained by the persistent compulsion to validate the dream ideology as a factual account when one was not able to realize the dream itself in action.

At later periods this original identification of dream and reality endured as a mixture, for, as early history shows, the accounts became a part of reality just as did the act, and the active hero tried to behave accordingly. The dream ideology not only reported dreamt deeds as though they had actually occurred, but such stories incited deeds which less strong-willed persons then reported as myths. These latter in turn set off dreams of similar deeds, which again were related as facts, and so on. All this, which a voluminous literature presents in detail, should only emphasize the view that the influence of the dream upon reality was at least as great as, and probably much more significant than, that of reality upon

[5] According to Ehrenreich: *General Mythology and its Ethnological Foundations* (Die allgemeine Mythologie und ihre ethnologischen Grundlegen), Leipzig, 1910, p. 149.

the dream. When one also considers that at primitive levels reality was about the same as the dream reality governed by animism and magic, the dream leads to the same conclusion as did the spiritual phenomenon studied previously: that what increasingly constitutes *reality* amounts to a proof, support, and expression of spiritual belief, or to an attempt to verify this belief by *making* it real.

But that excessive concretion of spiritual phenomena which became so crucial for scientific psychology was avenged here as elsewhere, for while the objective character of religion, state, and sexuality opposed their own symbolization, the subjective character of the dream restricted its objectification. In fairy tales and mythical motifs, the involvement of the Beyond in the Present led to misfortune, and the translation of dream reality into actual reality produced and did not avert the tragic death of the hero. Like the fairy-tale hero, the strong-willed individual was not content with taking the dream passively, but had to act it out and to perish in his attempt at immortality. He died because of that temporal desire for immortality which really signified the survival of his bodily self, and he needed to learn that there was no survival of the bodily self, but only a spiritual rebirth through collective symbols. Yet the dream as a purely subjective phenomenon seemed to bear out preanimistic belief in the bodily soul, and it has persisted as evidence for individual immortality in all stages of development of spiritual belief. This phenomenon created the immortal character of the hero, who seemed to a certain extent divine, invulnerable, and unconquerable, and was always saved by a miracle in the moments of greatest danger, during which he awoke from his fearful dream to return to real life and the certainties of the present. At the same time, the tendency to

101

make the self's dream-world immortality real led to all the misfortune of Nemesis and of inevitable, tragic death.

The best example of this sort of thing, which betrays the "morality" of all history and the myth as a verified dream narrative, seems to lie in a tale of the Winnebago Indians which Paul Radin[6] has rendered and analyzed most effectively. The hero of this unquestionably mythical narrative, which was told as though it were real, was called "Traveler" because he had wandered about the world since his earliest childhood. He was the only descendant of one of four great water spirits whom the supreme Earthmaker had created with his own hands and who was proud of this supernatural origin. On arriving home from his journey, the hero found his father in despair because he had learned that the arch-enemy of the water spirits was planning a war of annihilation against his tribe. The youth resolved to settle this conflict by a private duel with the enemy. He fasted to prepare himself for victory, and visited his water-spirit ancestors in the nether world. As the grandson of one of them, he received a blessing: "Grandson, I am going to give you a blessing. You are the first to receive one from me. Because you have made yourself suffer so much, because you have thirsted yourself to death, because you have made yourself a so truly compassion-inspiring spectacle, you shall attain to the full length of years. You shall die of old age. Remember that a normal life is very short. I was not born of a woman's womb, but Earthmaker molded me with his own hands." When the young man described this blessing to his father, the father replied: "My son, it is good. The water spirits are the greatest spirits in the world. You have had a good dream." Here

---

[6] *Primitive Man as Philosopher.* New York, 1927. See the chapter, "The Tragic Sense of Life."

the youth's experience with the water spirit was interpreted[7] as a dream caused by his transposed state and extended fast, which he apparently practiced not so much to steel himself for physical combat as to prove his superhumanity (immortality). Even such fasting did not seem to satisfy him, because he obviously wanted the water spirit to reassure him of his immortality, even though such a promise was not mentioned in the account cited. In another story of the same Indians (*loc. cit.*, p. 203), "The Faster," the son explained to the father that although a long life for himself, the death of his enemy, and the granting of all his wishes had all been guaranteed, he wanted to fast still longer in order to obtain realistic evidence of his immortality. ("But what I desire is never to die." The spirits could not dissuade him. "Indeed, I shall never be satisfied until I obtain the gift of immortal life," continued the boy. He was unable to face the thought of death; he dreaded it very much. In the council lodge of the spirits it was accordingly decided that he should die. So they looked down on the place where the boy was fasting, and there he lay dead.) It was as though he fasted and died to prove his immortality. The moral of this story was a warning to the young not to fast too long or to attempt the impossible. It is no mere truism that youth can gratify only those wishes that can be fulfilled.

A collective element prevailed in "The Traveler" in which the father and not the youth himself prompted the youth to fast longer, because it was only at his father's behest that the son decided to engage in a fatal conflict that would

[7] I do not know whether there is anything in the text available to me, which signifies that the gift-giving and wish-gratifying water spirit is designated as the Traveler, an identification which the dream character only serves to make more clear.

benefit only the tribe. Hence the final gift which the water spirit granted the youth for his many fasts was the annihilation of a whole village of the enemy, so that the youth would not be killed by them at least. The water spirit also promised the youth the right to prepare a "medicine" from the bones of the water spirit which would make him immortal.[8] But it turned out that the water spirit had promised more than he could deliver. The basis for his deceit lay in his declaration that he wanted to insure the youth's gratitude for help received against the water spirit's enemy. After much irresolution, the youth finally killed the enemy, but not before they had placed a curse on him which made their kinsmen kill him on his way home from the battle.

Again, death overtook the youth because he wanted immortality, and because the water spirit granted him the death of others, which only proved his mortality. Among many primitives like the Winnebagos, immortality meant that death was not brought about by natural causes but by some individual transgression. Of course, this causality was so broadly conceived that death was always inescapable. In the Winnebago myth of the twins, a mere fit of passion often sufficed to evoke punishment by the evil spirit. The individual offense originally signified a certain desire for immortality, but in the animistic era death came from an exaggerated tendency to translate into reality the ancient belief in the preanimistic bodily soul which the dream seemed to justify.

---

[8] In a third narrative, "The Seer" (*loc. cit.*, p. 196), the father prevails upon his son to fast in order to lengthen his own (the father's) life (rejuvenation wish). However, the father makes use of the water spirit's "medicine" only to kill others (in the final sense, the son), and therefore has to die. The tale of "The Traveler" retains only the father's ambition for his son, and seems to reconcile the paternal and filial immortality egoism.

Before we turn to the sexual era to see how the cause of death was transferred from an actualization of one's own immortal bodily soul (or dream-soul) to an abdication in favor of one's child, we should consider a feature of the original dream ideology which may help us to understand the mythical life of the hero. In the Winnebago narratives the individual and his immortality were dedicated to society and to altruism within the meaning of collective spiritual belief. This dedication, which was a sacrifice from which the individual at times sought to escape by leaving the group, was symbolized more clearly by Traveler than by the classical heroes who tried to escape the spiritual demands for socialization by setting forth on adventures that promised personal immortality. Yet this escape always led to death. In the sense of dream ideology, Traveler, whose strife for immortality so clearly betrayed such a retreat from social duty, seems to symbolize the wandering soul which leaves the sleeping body to roam beyond space and time. Hence the mythical hero who possibly portrayed the independent and immortal dream ego, or soul, was compelled to pursue his own destiny even when it meant only his death and a mythical immortality.

As a transition to the sexual era, in which the individual abandoned his bodily immortality for a procreative one, we may cite the early Babylonian legend of the divine human, Gilgamesh, and his mortal friend, Eabani. Both ideologies seem to be embodied in these two friends and their destinies, while Utnapishti, the ancestor who warned of the Deluge, corresponded to the immortal water spirit. Following the death of his friend Eabani, Gilgamesh renounced himself to Utnapishti in order to gain immortality for himself, just as the Indian youth had done to the water spirit. His fast was

105

not deliberate, for he was unable to find food on his difficult journey from the waters of the dead, and, after he had eaten at the bidding of Utnapishti's wife, he fell asleep from fatigue (death sleep). Although this journey into the nether world in which Gilgamesh failed to find immortality was not related as a dream, like all dreams motivated by myths, the story betrays its dream character even in the absence of explicit evidence to that effect.

There was the significant dream in which Gilgamesh learned of the arrival of the plainsman, Eabani, who was determined to be the hero's mortal friend, brother, and comrade in arms:

> Once he dreamt how in the starlight a star fell upon him like a host of the heavenly deity, Anu; how he could not shake off this burden because of its greater strength; how he finally clove to it as he would to a woman and then laid it at the feet of his wise mother, Reshat-Belit, who made it equal to Gilgamesh. In a second dream there appeared to him a man whom—like the star in the first dream—he laid at the feet of his mother, whom he likewise pressed to himself, and whom his mother likewise made his equal. Both phenomena symbolized his future friend and beloved companion, Eabani, and since this concerned Erekh, Gilgamesh addressed him and brought the two together in friendship.[9]

This dream forecast the future because the magic-minded person had to translate it into reality.[10] The fact that we are

[9] Quoted from P. Jensen: *The Gilgamesh Epic in World Literature* (Der Gilgamesch-Epos in der Weltliteratur). Vol. I, 1906, p. 7.

[10] Later (*op. cit.*, pp. 583 f), Jensen makes it plausible that these dreams were reported in the Book of Kings (I, 17) as actual occurrences, and indeed in Elias's awakening from the dead: "With this he laid the lifeless body of the widow's son on Elias's bed, lay on him thrice at full length so as to bring him to life, and then gave him over to his mother."

concerned with two quite similar dreams occurring the same night offers us differing cues which lead us further into the spiritual meaning of the material, and disclose its relevance to the emerging sexual era. The involvement of the mother in both the dream and its interpretation signified her consent to the hero's new son and brother. Her interpretation superseded her own conception- and birth-dream which Gilgamesh dreamt twice (as it were, for her), and which was to be attributed to her only in the fully developed sexual era. I do not mean that the Babylonians had displaced the dream from the mother to the son, any more than I believe that Gilgamesh's dream signified concealed incest with his mother, although the dream made Gilgamesh the creator of Eabani, whom the mother simply accepted in her interpretation to her son. The characteristic feature of this animistic dream material is exactly that Gilgamesh created Eabani by waking him from the dead, as God created man, and not by begetting him as a father does his son. Hence Gilgamesh was two-thirds a god, and in a sense stood nearer to immortality than did the mortal Eabani whom he created as a representation of his mortal Double.

This whole conception is confirmed by Eabani's fate, and by the motivation of his mortality, which already betrayed the influence of sexual ideology. Undisturbed by earthly cares and human knowledge, Eabani lived a paradisiacal life with the desert animals until the hunters whom he had driven from the desert got their revenge upon him. From the temple of Ishtar these hunters fetched one Hierolule, who seduced Eabani and robbed him of his "innocence." The animals then fled him; he found no peace in the city and cursed all women as the cause of his downfall. He had fearful premonitions and dreams of death, which were soon

PSYCHOLOGY AND THE SOUL

followed by his actual death. Gilgamesh then lamented Eabani's death as though it were his own—which it did symbolize, because Gilgamesh's mortal counterpart was lost with Eabani's death, and because his immortal self remained in perpetual fear of death until he perished in search of immortality. In the narrative, Eabani's spirit appeared in order to manifest the will of the gods, and to *cause* and not merely to announce Gilgamesh's death.

In contrast with Eabani and Adam, the hero of the sexual era who succumbed to sexual temptation and lost his immortality, Gilgamesh resisted the temptations of Ishtar:

> "Come now, my Gilgamesh, make love to me! Give me a child by thee! Be my husband and let me be thy wife," so spake she to him and urged her suit with glowing words. But he remembered her past, her faithlessness in love, and the misfortunes which all her lovers had suffered. She had already lain with five others, and had caused them all to suffer in some way. . . . The sixth, Ishullanu, her father's gardener, whom she had asked to dine with her but who had scornfully rejected her, was struck down by her and confined like an animal so that he could not move. (Jensen, pp. 17 f.)

But abstinence from intercourse was as pernicious for Gilgamesh as giving in to seduction had been for the others. For the scorned Ishtar sent a powerful "celestial bull" which wounded Eabani, who then had to die because he killed the bull. On the next day Eabani dreamt of his death and acquired an illness that became fatal twelve days later. The thoroughly frightened Gilgamesh then cried, "Could not I, as he, lay me to rest and never arise throughout all eternity?"

Thus at the beginning of the sexual era this story of

Gilgamesh shows clearly how the heroic myth sprang from animistic tales which related the dream as true, and sought to transpose its hero into reality. The hero's brother (or sibling) role characteristic of fabulous dream motifs represents the hero's mortal Double or bodily soul of the dream. This role also symbolized the passivity of the hero, to whom everything *happened* as in a dream, and it symbolized his stupidity, his inexperience, and his naïve adherence to ancient spiritual belief which the mythical hero had lost by his acceptance of sexual knowledge and ideology. The mythical hero stood alone, and had no helper, guardian spirit, or Double. But since his nature was partly divine and partly human, he incorporated both mortal and immortal souls within himself. The hero of the spiritual era perished in his attempt to realize immortality in the form of perpetual life. The hero of the sexual era relinquished immortality to his descendants, and achieved it through his children. The Gilgamesh epic juxtaposed and embodied these two ideologies in the hero and his Double, with Gilgamesh meeting his fate in terms of the surviving animistic ideology, and Eabani his through the new sexual ideology. At the same time, the myth shows that one could no longer deny sexuality, because abstinence involved the same danger of death as did intercourse.[11] However, it is significant that the original

[11] One of the rare primitive narratives which denies the reality of dreams (*i.e.,* immortality of the soul), deals with an infringement of a sexual prohibition. This unusual dream story, which concerns a legend of the Kpellese and is reported by D. Westermann in *A Negro Tribe in Liberia* (Ein Negerstamm in Liberia, pp. 457 f), indicates only in the final sentence that the events which appeared in the dream were not real: "What he dreamt was imaginary. Had the young man's dream been real anything that anyone dreams would be real." Kpana, the hero of the story, was enjoined by his friends to go fishing. He ate, and then slept so heavily against his fish basket that the others could not waken him, and the

cause of death was not sexuality as defined by the Bible and Western morality, but the very egoistic wish for immortality which governed sexual resistance, in relation to which sexuality was interpreted as sin. Adam perished because of his wish for immortality, and not because of sexuality, which was actually imposed on Eve and him as a duty. This is clear even in the biblical account as long as one does not follow the spiritual line of the Church in interpreting sexuality as sin. Eating the forbidden fruit amounted to gaining the tree of life, or the "medicine," and should have rendered sexuality superfluous because it made the original egoistic immortality possible. All doubt as to this conception of the "fall from grace" is precluded by an ancient Sumerian parallel[12] to the biblical story, which, as far as the incomplete text allows, construes the real offense as being the struggle for immortality, without once mentioning sexual temptation and "sin." Although man ate of the divine fruit and was driven from the garden into the desert, the end of the text says that he did not therefore fall into sin but reached a higher plane of existence. He did not get "the reed that frees from death" any more than did the youth in Traveler, but he acquired

basket on his back befouled his clothing. He dreamed that he came to the king of another city who offered Kpana his daughter on the condition that he would not return home. The Rock, which had the role of dream god, presented him with a rich nuptial gift for his bride, but made his possession of his beloved and her country dependent on the condition that he lie with the girl for eight days without indulging in the sexual act. But on the seventh day Kpana succumbed to the girl's enticements. Then Kpana awoke from his dream and looked back at his fouled clothing. The long, deep sleep and the fouling are unequivocal symbols of death as punishment for failing to abstain from the sexual act, or for failing to abstain spiritually, which makes the dream untrue.

[12] *Cf.* Edw. Chiera: "A Sumerian Tablet Relating to the Fall of Man." *The American Journal of Semitic Languages and Literatures.* Vol. XXXIX, No. 1, Oct. 1922.

a large portion of worldly goods. "Humanity, thou art to know abundance!" On the basis of what has already been covered, this closing statement may be understood to mean that man should give up his hope for immortality and turn his interests to his present life. This narrative, which in other respects concerned a race more than an individual, clearly states that man's punishment was not the loss of his immortality, which he had never had in the first place, but of his earthly life and the happiness it could have held for him had his search for immortality not robbed him of it.

This Sumerian text emphasizes the motif of *eating* which also plays a prominent role in the biblical story, the epic of Gilgamesh, and the myth of the Winnebagos. The Sumerian tablet portrayed man as being driven from the heavenly fields with the words: "Go, till the garden, raise food for eating! Thou shalt never reach me (the food of God)." And then: ". . . since the hand of the sons of the menials has reached the food, their eyes have been opened . . ." he receives a wealth of nourishment from the beasts and the fields. The biblical account interpreted the agricultural motif as a curse. But, after being banished from the realm of the immortals, the hero of the Gilgamesh epic received bread from Utnapishti's wife and, according to Utnapishti's instructions, gathered a plant from the lake, which corresponded to the bread of eternal life. However, this plant only protected the hero from the immediate dangers and rescued him from a serpent. It must be noted that Gilgamesh did not eat the plant as soon as he found it, because it was food for the soul rather than for the body. When we relate this insight to the ritual fasts of primitives and to their magical concept of eating as an incorporation of soul-stuff (Mana), we have to recognize in all these myths a warning that man

111

should direct his attention more to earthly sustenance than to spiritual food, or that he should at least relate food and nourishment to physical rather than religious motives. However, as the Faster shows, this spiritual nourishment and immortalizing food of the gods really signified the superhuman ability to live without earthly nourishment. Apparently the acceptance of sexuality as a means to procreative immortality had an influence on this practical side of nourishment, because it involved a strong motive to compensate for the loss of spiritual power resulting from the sexual act by an ingestion of nourishment that was superior in kind and quantity. However, it seems to me that the irrelevance of earthly nourishment for independent survival of the soul also stemmed from the dream, for the widespread custom of placing food and other necessities of life in the grave with the dead belonged to a preanimistic belief that the body-soul could not survive apart from the body and its welfare. At the animistic stage of spiritual belief, fasting corresponded to sleep, and eating was an "awakening symptom" which warmed the dreamer of his mortality, but also showed him that he still lived and had not fallen asleep forever.

Like other realistic culture phenomena, the transition from natural nourishment (fruit and game) to cattle breeding and agriculture is explicable largely in terms of spiritual ideology. The traditions cited above, which portray the transition from the spiritual to the sexual era, also disclose the relation of the spiritual era to natural nourishment (paradise), and of the sexual era to the cultivation of food. It is as though man had first to know and recognize sexuality for itself before he could utilize procreation and fertilization in plants and animals for his own ends. This is both the biblical "knowledge" and, according to the Sumerian text, the progress

112

which man makes both by exchanging individual for procreative immortality and by enriching his earthly life through an abundance of food, clothing, and other goods.[13] But this "application" of sexual knowledge, which signified an exaggerated personal goal and was symbolized[14] by agriculture and stockbreeding, finally led to worldly luxury, gluttony, and lust, and allowed man to forget spirituality and his future life.

This collapse of the first concretion of sexual ideology simulated the myth of the great flood, which was the first epic of mankind because it comprehended the fate of an entire people rather than of a single individual. In this legend everything perished because of sexuality in the sense of the new ideology, and ceased to multiply merely by expansion of the group. This epic, which the Bible related as fact, also appears in the Gilgamesh legend of Utnapishti, which explains how a hero as well as a human being could be excluded from the realm of the spiritual gods. Yet the flood really seems to be a dream product, and not just a

[13] Gilgamesh, who came to Utnapishti starved and naked, received nourishment (bread) and a beautiful garment which never wore out (hence Adam and Eve's leaf garments which were supplanted by hides, and natural fruits which were supplanted by cultivated ones). Agriculture derived personal possession from sexual ideology, since the possession of agricultural goods, as of a child, was a result of one's own activity. In the presexual era, the natural pasture lands had belonged to the community or commonwealth. Gilgamesh knew no better than to kill the celestial bull which Ishtar had sent with her love, and to make a weapon of its horns. In contrast, how noble a stockbreeder seemed Jacob with his speckled lambs!

[14] See my *Psychoanalytic Contributions to the Study of Myths* (Psychoanalytische Beiträge zur Mythenforschung) Second edition, 1922, Chapter II: "Symbolism" (Die Symbolik), especially 28 ff. In Chapter IV, on "The Significance of the Deluge Saga" (Zur Deutung der Sintflutsage) I have also indicated the dream origin of the great flood, by referring to individual dreams.

113

story. When the gods had decided to destroy the city by a flood, Ea, the god of the deep, sent Utnapishti a dream which warned him: "Thou, man of Shurippak, son of Upar-Tutu! Build a shelter! Build a ship! Forget thy worldly wealth; look to thy life! Bring all manner of beings into this ship!" The story means that Gilgamesh was shown how man could win immortality not by actively seeking it in his own way, but in the way of the passive mythical hero to whom the gods disclosed the immortal soul in a dream. According to spiritual ideology, this means that man escaped from a too realistic sexual era into a dream which reassured him that his corporeal soul existed, and that he remained immortal in spite of his acceptance of the sexual ideology.

Before we turn to the classical Oedipus myth of the sexual era, which discloses the transition to the type of dream analysis characteristic of the psychological era, I may summarize the foregoing findings with respect to the various forms of epic narrative. The fairy tale as the earliest form of narrative corresponds to the preanimistic equivalence of dream and reality, in which the dream was narrated as a working reality. This was possible because its ideology agreed throughout with the magical world view. The Odyssey was the finest example of this narrative which persisted into the heroic, sexual era without losing its dream character. Odysseus was the passive dream hero to whom everything happened—favorably, of course—in a dream. His salvation from all the threats of death in the lower world and from all the dangers of sexuality in the upper world are so patently significant for the question of immortality that the point needs only to be mentioned.

In contrast to the fairy tale, the heroic myth of ancient civilized peoples belonged to a phase of the sexual era in which dreams were no longer told as reality but were relived by an *active* hero in real life. A myth portrays not only a hero's superhuman efforts to win immortality, but the fruitlessness of these efforts as well, and it ends tragically, in contrast to the fairy tale which ends happily. That the mythical dream was true only when it could be translated into reality was consistent with the realization of immortality in the hereafter. The Grecian Oedipus saga was the purest type of this legend, because it tried to put sexual ideology directly at the service of personal immortality. In contrast to the spiritual ideology of the fairy tale, the mythical hero stood alone, because in his mortal and immortal respects he represented the spiritual Double that had originated in dream ideology.

The epic differed from these two narrative types in dealing with the fate of whole peoples. This is consistent with the view that even the sexual era's collective immortality, which was embodied in the group and manifested in collective consciousness, offered no satisfactory solution for the problem of individuality. Through its efforts to assert itself as an expanding power, a people may perish in just such a collective, procreative struggle for personal immortality. The classical example of the folk epic, which portrays this collective and ineffective strife for concrete spiritual and sexual immortality, is the Iliad.

Fairy tales quite properly treated the dream as a *present* experience. In myths the dream determined *future* behavior, because its sexual ideology of immortality first had to be translated into reality. The epic portrayed the hero's dreamt fate as a *past* event, because the old dream ideology could no longer cope with current events, and because it could only console man for the fact that good times had come and

115

gone. Thus a poet served his disillusioned people by going back to the mythical dream form for the bodily soul as a consolation against "murderous" war.

We now come to the psychological era, in which the dream acquired a "wish fulfilling" function not by virtue of its content, as Freud would say, but by virtue of the dream itself, irrespective even of its Freudian "latent" content, which is not spiritual but merely psychological. The dream itself did not concern wishes that could be fulfilled, but spiritual ones that could not be fulfilled. It showed man the soul that was independent of his body, and it was the dream as such and not its particular content that did this. The anxiety dream was an exception, in which the self escaped from its fear of mortality by awakening from a death-like sleep.[15] Other than anxiety dreams served to prolong sleep, not in a psychological sense of providing gratification (Freud) but in the spiritual sense of demonstrating immortality. Anxiety dreams interrupted sleep when it came too near to death and threatened the feeling of immortality. Both types of dream served to deny death; the one, by positively evoking the dreamer's own bodily soul and the souls of dead or absent persons; and in the other, negatively, by rescuing the dreamer from deathlike sleep. Thus *dreaming* itself became a denial of death, because it *always proved that one still survived and had not fallen into one's final sleep.*

It is characteristic that Freud's psychological dream in-

---

[15] "For 'dreaming' and for 'being half dead' East African natives use the same expression, 'drokuku'"; from Ig. Jezower: *The Book of Dreams* (Das Buch der Träume), Berlin 1928, p. IX. Also, among primitives, sleep and death are closely related conceptually as well as linguistically; see F. Scherke, *On the Behavior of Primitives Regarding Death* (Ueber das Verhalten Primitiven zum Tode), Langensalza, 1923, p. 212.

terpretation, which was based on the ideology of wish fulfillment, avoided the problem of the anxiety dream, ostensibly because this type of dream concerned the unsolved problem of neurotic anxiety. However, this anxiety corresponded to a death anxiety like that of the dream, and it precluded psychological interpretation because the dream was spiritual. Because man's wish for immortality made death incomprehensible to him as a natural phenomenon, the dream was as "causeless" as the death for which he had to find new causes at every stage of spiritual belief. In this sense, primitive man's original "explanation" of death was the most nearly correct because it was spiritual and not causal: the individual brought about his own death by insisting that his immortality be transformed into reality. The reinterpretation of this explanation in the sense of sexual ideology, which blamed sex for death, still governs our whole Western morality through the concept of sin, on which the psychoanalytic explanation of anxiety and guilt was based. Freud's attempt to subordinate the anxiety dream to the theory of wish fulfillment, which interpreted anxiety as a displaced wish, was always unsatisfactory even to Freud. Particularly because of the "death symbolism" of dreams which Stekel[16] has stressed, and because of the theory of anxiety presented in my *Trauma of Birth (Trauma der Geburt)*, this theory of wish fulfillment has become untenable.

There may be differentiated, then, two groups of dreams which the ancients' motives and "imagination" led them to differentiate in relation to their particular spiritual ideology as real and "god given," respectively, since, on the one hand,

---

[16] Wilhelm Stekel: *The Language of the Dream* (Die Sprache des Traumes), Wiesbaden, 1911.

primitive man believed that while he slept his soul voluntarily left his body and visited living or dead persons and, on the other, that the souls of absent or dead persons came to him almost against his wishes. These were pleasant and unpleasant dreams, or wish- and anxiety-dreams in the psychological sense. The former reassured the dreamer that his own soul was a being independent of his body because it wandered about as it pleased; and, in reminding him of dead persons, the latter forewarned him of his mortality. Homer differentiated "light" and "dark" dreams, which corresponded to the higher and lower worlds depicted by many dreams in the Iliad. Such dreams were either divine apparitions which called upon humans to act and warned them of impending action, or human manifestations of the spirits of the dead. Therefore, these two groups of dreams were oriented respectively to the future and the present, or to the soul's immortality and mortality. An attempt to make anxiety dreams subject to the wish for an immortal soul seems recognizable in the newer idea that all dreams should be god-given and therefore prophetic, as were the dead who often appeared in dreams. "Those seeking counsel had to enter a certain temple or go to a cleft in the rocks (for example, in Pytho) whence flowed stimulating vapors, and to fall into a sleep during which certain dream apparitions offered them instruction. In place of the dark Earth goddess, Gaia, there followed later the radiant Apollo, god of light, and the inspired dreamer on whom the Delphic oracle bestowed this unique power became an important follower of the Apollonian cult."[17] Thus, as Rohde has so convincingly

[17] L. Binswanger: *Changes in Dream Conceptualization and Interpretation, from the Greeks up to the Present Day* (Wandlungen in der Auffassung und Deutung des Traumes von den Griechen bis zur Gegenwart), Berlin 1928.

shown in his book *Psyche*,[18] the Greek spiritual cult and belief in immortality influenced both divine affairs and important worldly events. Like the primitive fast, this temple sleep, which made a seeker of counsel receptive to dreams and their interpretation, gave way during the fifth century B.C. to dream books and tables which stipulated prophecies and warnings to be drawn from dream images and symbols. This kind of dream interpretation came from Egypt, the land of mantic and death cults, and, like the longing for immortality of the soul, has survived even in current superstitions.

In contrast, the scientific concern with dreams has had only a relatively short history, and has produced very few ideas not already anticipated in the spiritual approach to dreams. Aristotle[19] may be cited again, even though Hippocrates and Artemidorus[20] had pointed out the relation of dreams to the dreamer's experiences, personal relations, and bodily processes. Aristotle was the first to try to give a physiology and psychology of dreams related to the sense organs, "in so far as he sought to explain dreams not as events external to man himself but as necessary manifestations of the human spirit." (Binswanger) As psychoanalysis has since tried to do, Artemidorus sought to combine psycho-

[18] Erwin Rohde: *Psyche. Grecian Spiritual Cults and Belief in Immortality* (Psyche. Seelenkult und Unsterblichkeitsglaube der Griechen), 1893, 9th and 10th editions, Tübingen, 1925.

[19] *Minor scientific writings* (Kleine naturwiss. Schriften), Leipzig, 1924. See especially, "Sleeping and Waking" (Vom Schlafen und Wachen), "Dreams (Von den Träumen), and "Prophetic dreams" (Von den weissagenden Träumen).

[20] Artemidorus of Daldis: *Symbolism of dreams* (Symbolik der Träume), Translated and annotated by Fr. S. Krauss, Vienna, 1881. (Hans Licht has translated the sexual portions of this work in Volume IX of *Anthropophytera*.)

119

logical and symbolic dream interpretation by explaining all dreams in terms of the individual psyche instead of the gods, and it was this scientific conception which led ultimately to Freud's substitution of two kinds of interpretation for two kinds of dream. Artemidorus also distinguished between meaningful dreams, which forecast the future, and those which were meaningless, subjective in origin, and allied with actual bodily and psychic stimuli (Freud's "diurnal remnants"). But since dream content could not always be explained even in relation to a primitive world view, Artemidorus further divided meaningful dreams into those which portrayed the event as it actually would occur with the same persons in the dream, and into those which portrayed the future allegorically and required a more sophisticated interpretation. The belief that dreams which portray events according to their actual nature forbode good, clearly reflects a "psychological" interpretation of the old identity of dream and reality. On the other hand, Artemidorus was the first to group dreams systematically according to the objects which they portrayed (birth, death, sexuality, bodily members, occupation, etc.), and thus to establish a dream typology.

According to Freud's own statements, these typical dreams which recur in the same or similar ways with most individuals, have opposed Freud's theory of individual analysis, just as the anxiety dream deprived him of his theory of wish fulfillment. One should not be surprised then to find old spiritual material worked over in the content of typical dreams, for whose interpretation Freud had to refer to mythology and cultural history. That the water dream symbolized birth and death, and always rescued the dreamer from an actually nonexistent danger, should of itself suffice to indicate the spiritual import of the dream in the sense of immortality ideology, in contrast to psychological interpretation in the sense of wish fulfillment. The reference of this type of dream to the "unconscious" wish of childhood was only a restatement of the incomprehensible soul concept in psychological terms. The dream of being nude, which Freud explained by an adult compulsion based on infantile exhibitionistic pleasure, may have a birth ("birthday clothes") as well as a death interpretation (compare the undressing of Gilgamesh upon his entrance into the nether regions); and actually the episode in the Odyssey which Freud cited by way of comparison, in which the hero awoke from his sleep naked and covered with mud in the presence of Nausicaa, was a miraculous salvation from death to a new life, such as occurred several times in the Odyssey. As elsewhere, Freud made the sexual element in this episode the sole basis for its interpretation. Thus, in the first edition of his *Interpretation of Dreams,* Freud treated typical dreams as reproductions of the child's pleasurable sensations from swinging or rocking, but explained them later by reference to birds as sexual symbols of masculine potency.[21] Yet again, in the first edition of *Interpretation of Dreams* (p. 175), one encounters the dream by a four-year-old girl, in which Freud interpreted her playmates' flying away as a death symbol only because it enabled him to show the little egoist's death wish against her sister and relatives, who as angels, all flew away in her dream. Disregarding the fact that a child's normal egoism demands vehicles of play just as often as it rejects them, perhaps the deeper egoism of the dream consists of the wish that even though one were dead one would not be entirely so, and that if one had wings

[21] In this instance he rests on Dr. Paul Feder's interpretation of the sensation of flying as an autosymbolic representation of erection.

one could come back to play as well as to live. Freud even comprehended the dream of the death of loved ones as a fulfillment of the death wish which was valid for oneself (1st edition, p. 172), and which he misplaced onto the weakness of childhood without resolving the resultant difficulties of the misplacement or really explaining the dream. He had to limit the death wish of the child against his elders to those of the same sex, and then to "interpret" spiritual symbols (immortality ideology) psychologically as jealousy in the sense of sexual ideology. He believed he had found the sanction for this interpretation in the fable of Oedipus, who unwittingly killed his father, married his own mother, and perished when he discovered his crime.

However, this downfall of Oedipus was no more a punishment for incest and patricide than Adam's death was a punishment for sexual intercourse. It was not a "punishment" at all, but one of the numerous "causal explanations" of death, whose inevitability man could not accept and therefore wanted to deny in order to gain immortality. Only in contrast to primitives (Traveler), Oedipus did not seek immortality in the sense of belief in an individual corporeal soul as Gilgamesh and Achilles had done, by invoking the Doubles and shades of departed friends, but, in the sense of the new sexual era, by denying his father and wanting to be reborn in his mother. Like all other heroes, Oedipus died trying to achieve immortality.

Freud explained this spiritual myth psychologically in terms of the so-called sexual relation of the child to his elders, in which the child wanted to possess the member of the opposite sex and therefore turned his jealous hatred against the member of the same sex. In this example we can readily detect the emergence of psychology from spiritual

122

belief. The imminent objection that the animistic view was essentially a prescientific interpretation of the same facts which psychoanalysis has explained psychologically, breaks down in relation to the clear primacy of the immaterial and unreal. The accounts of incestuous relations among natural and civilized peoples are particularly well suited to support this view, for like primitive group relations they are social manifestations of collective spirituality, or, as in the highly developed states of the sexual era, they are the purest examples of actualization of spiritual ideology by deeds that may be found in dreams. Thus the incest dream to which the legend of Oedipus refers was not the result of repressed incestuous wishes. Instead, actual incest was the result of actualizing the dream, in which the wish was not to possess the mother but to prove the ego's ideology of spiritual immortality.

The Oedipus fable belonged to a phase of the sexual era in which the individual who was striving for immortality learned that the dream could no longer be translated into reality because the ancient spiritual belief necessary to this translation had to be abandoned. The position of Sophocles in *Oedipus* (see p. 995 of Donner's translation), in which the mother mentioned the hero's incest dream, seems to me to support this point. "For many men see themselves associated with their mothers in their dreams. Yet whoever regards this as meaningless bears the burden of life easily." This remark was no mere consoling reference to the typicality of the dream in question, but a warning to Oedipus to accommodate himself to the ruling ideology which no longer allowed him to make the dream true in order to substantiate spiritual belief, and suggested rather that he regard the dream as inconsequential. Oedipus answered with the hint that all would be very well if his mother had not actually been alive, *i.e.*, had he not translated his experience into reality. In this connection it was significant that the mother, as a concrete incarnation of the sexual era, controverts the validity of this dream, which should have been the experience of a masculine dreamer.[22] Moreover, Jakaste brings the mother's point of view into relation with a general world view expressed in the Oedipus saga,[23] which incited one to live according to the manifest character of reality without trying to explain it causally.[24]

The Oedipus fable allows one to show not only how physiological interpretation grew out of spiritual belief, but also how the concretely inclined ideology of the sexual era served to give psychology a biological foundation. The sexual interpretation of the Oedipus saga was not original with Freud, but was an interpretation of spiritual belief in the sense of the ideology of the sexual era. Although its deep latent meaning was spiritual, Freud tried to interpret it psychobiologically. His attempt was paradigmatic of all psychoanalysis, which has interpreted spiritual phenomena of the sexual era in psychobiological terms. There is certainly no question that such an interpretation is possible, but the complete absence of methodological separation of these various categories of differing importance has led to the formidable confusion of spiritual phenomena, biological facts, and

---

[22] In *Dawn* (Morgenröte), Nietzsche erroneously ascribes this hint to the hero himself: "Wise Oedipus already knew how to take comfort in the thought that one can do nothing about his dreams."

[23] *Truth and Reality* (Wahrheit und Wirklichkeit), p. 33. Also, "The analytic reaction" (Die analytische Reaktion), pp. 67 f.

[24] Jakaste: "What needs man to fear, who depends upon chance and foresees nothing? Know only what is; to live is best: fear nought of thy mother's marriage."

psychological concepts, which is evident in Freud's attempts at dream interpretation.

This is best seen in the symbolism which the psychoanalytic interpreter of dreams invokes when the dreamer's individual material fails to explain a dream, *i.e.*, when the psychological interpretation breaks down because it fails to apply to the spiritual material which is the essence of the dream. Freud committed the same methodological error when he invoked the sexual interpretation that the symbol had acquired in the sexual era. After all, it was not Freud who first interpreted the symbol sexually, for man had already done that in the sexual era. Freud only (mis-) took this sexual interpretation for the original phenomenon, and then proceeded to interpret it psychobiologically without recognizing that he was merely rephrasing the sexualized spiritual ideology in scientific terms and was utterly failing to consider the basic spiritual phenomenon which required for its understanding something other than a sexual or psychological interpretation.

Now this psychological interpretation, which rested on the consoling ideology of "free association," had nothing to do with the dream as such, but belonged to a later discussion of psychic causality (see the last chapter, below) whose methodological status I have already questioned.[25] And, as Freud himself admitted, the purely psychological part of his *Interpretation of Dreams* yielded nothing characteristic of the dream itself, but only matters of general psychological significance, such as the mechanisms of transference, condensation, symbolism, etc. In the *Interpretation*, and more definitely in the "Id," Freud ascribed these mech-

[25] See especially, "The analytic reaction" (Die analytische Reaktion), Second Section: "Past and present" (Vergangenheit und Gegenwart), 47 ff.

anisms to the unconscious, and so merely rephrased the spiritual psychologically. Symbolic and anxiety dreams, which resist interpretation in terms of any individual psychology of the self, show this most clearly because they can be understood only in relation to that "unconscious" which never becomes conscious, and which Jung has properly called "collective" because of its identity with the spiritual. The typical sexual symbols of serpent, mouse, and bird originally had spiritual meanings, and it was only this characteristic which made them useful in the sexual era's new ideology. Freud then biologized them, as Stekel biologized the spiritual ideology in his "death symbolism," without denying the broad aspects of the death problem. Thus psychoanalytic interpretation of dreams faced the antithesis of death and sexuality, which corresponds to the concepts of guilt and punishment of the Fall through Sin,[26] but without having first considered its underlying immortality ideology.

However, all extra-symbolic materials which free association brings to light in the dream content are not unconscious but "preconscious." That is, they are individual ideas having only a psychological meaning; they are unrelated to the other-worldly, spiritual, or "divine" content which underlies consciousness, and of which there is a trace in Freud's high regard both for the "depth" of the unconscious and for the interpretation of dreams as such. However, Freud turned this depth into a superficial thing, because he interpreted in the terms of natural science psychology that which he failed to recognize as spiritual in the already concretized

---

[26] The comprehensive presentation by N. P. Williams: *The Ideas of the Fall and of Original Sin* (London, 1927) attempts to show the origin of these ideas in Judaism, and traces the development which they experienced under Christianity.

126

form of the sexual ideology. But this psychological explanation of dreams completely failed to be an explanation because one interprets all conscious contents psychologically
in the same way and not as just momentarily conscious, but
as something capable of mutual involvement with any other
content that can become conscious. The state of sleep, which
is the single fact characteristic of the dream, remained the
same for Freud as it had been for Aristotle. But just as
Aristotle's original psychology of dreams found it hard to
separate itself from Plato's spiritual doctrine, and just as
Aristotle tried to supplant Plato's belief in the prophetic
character of dreams with his own psychophysiological explanations, so in his high regard for the dream as a portrayal
of the unconscious, and in spite of his own intentions, Freud
came after all to honor the ancient spiritual interpretation
and to invite the criticism of all natural scientists, who like
Freud condemned these ancient beliefs as superstitions.

The new respect for the dream was Freud's only real contribution to the dream problem, both because he rescued
it from the insignificance thrust upon it by experimental and
sensory-physiological psychology, and because he gave it a
deep interpretation which revealed not the unconscious but
only the ancient spiritual beliefs. Freud's other contributions
had nothing to do with the nature of the dream, for they
comprised a psychology derived from the dream phenomenon by interpretation, and not by an understanding of a
spiritually won science. In order to substantiate this claim
we should consider the significance of the *Interpretation of
Dreams* for general psychology as well as for the development of Freudian psychology. It appears to me beyond
question that the volume published in 1900 represented the
standard work on psychoanalysis in a sense other than that

127

which Freud intended. I see in the *Interpretation* the beginning of the true Freudian psychoanalysis, which one may
regard as originating historically with Breuer, as Freud
averred, which actually became allied psychologically with
Breuer, and which was more Freud's own personal creation
than was the version of psychoanalysis appearing in his
Interpretation of Dreams. Apart from its psychoanalytic significance, the psychological orientation inherent in the *Interpretation of Dreams* represents a decisive turning point
in the development of scientific psychology, not so much by
virtue of the information it provides as by the tendencies
which it betrays.

By scientific criteria, the Freudian *Interpretation of Dreams*
signifies a marked advance in the realm of subjective psychology, because it made the dreamer both the subject and object
of psychological observation. The "observer" was excluded
and, as Freud noted in his preface, the inner life of the person investigated was exposed to the scrutiny of outsiders to
a degree yet unheard of in natural science. On the face of
it, this remarkable attitude on Freud's part should have been
able to disarm almost any critic, because it made Freud appear
not to be placing any personal interest in an analysis of the
father of psychoanalysis above the facts. But we are obliged
to be more critical and to look at the *Interpretation of Dreams*
objectively, not only because such objectivity should have
been hard for its author to attain, but also because it constitutes the only way of understanding the psychoanalytic
theory based on the *Interpretation of Dreams,* and of enabling
anyone to evaluate its significance for psychological science.
We must be critical because this very personal material was
used in the book to portray and establish a general scientific
interpretation of dreams. As other critics have noted, this

book was a greater contribution to dream interpretation than to dream analysis;[27] it was a psychology of dreams, but a psychology which at its best left dreams unexplained. The interpretation of dreams never was and never can be scientific, even when a complete psychological analysis underlies it. Interpretation is always spiritual because it has always yielded, and still yields, meanings which conform to various spiritual ideologies; and between it and psychological analysis there exists a gap which cannot be bridged for many types of dream, a gap which is inherent in the problem of the dream, and which brings a dualism to the *Interpretation of Dreams* which Freud tried but only failed to mask.

In the foreword to the second edition of the *Interpretation of Dreams* (1909) Freud gave a hint of this dualism of which he was unaware when he wrote the book: "I believe it to be a part of my self-analysis and a reaction to the death of my father, which is the most significant event and the most incisive deprivation in the life of a man." With the first edition this personal insight which was mentioned so casually had already become the basis for Freud's entire psychoanalytic psychology, and it survives as such today. In this quotation Freud declared the subjective source of his psychology, just as though he had established the universality of the father complex independently of it and would now verify placidly that the theory held in his own case as well. Certainly the subjective origin of an idea does not detract from any objective validity which it may otherwise prove to have. But it is obvious that the general validity of the Freudian thesis is to be disputed. Even in psychoanalysis, daily experi-

[27] For example, Kuno Mattenzwey: "A study in exposition and criticism of the Freudian theory of neuroses" (Versuch zu einer Darstellung und Kritik der Freudschen Neurosenlehre), *Zeitschr. f. Pathopsychologie*, vol. 1, 1912.

ence shows that the death of one's father is not necessarily the most important event in the life of a man, but that it may often be an extremely minor one. I even venture to assert that the death of Freud's father was not the most important event of his life prior to his writing of the *Interpretation of Dreams*. The question why Freud then believed in the importance of his father's death and should have predicted it for all human experience leads us deeper into the problem of psychology than does any theoretical study of dreams.

We must first relate to this belief of Freud the psycho-analytically suggested doubt whether and to what degree a person's declarations about himself approximate psychological truth. Freud's own analyses have taught us to be skeptical of these assertions which gain their most important ends by a compulsive displacement of the analysee's attention. Freud achieved this particular insight through his analyses of his own dreams, not immediately, as one might expect, but a few years later when he began to revise the book for a new edition. In the meantime he had worked the Oedipus complex which had dominated the *Interpretation of Dreams* into the core of his psychology, and for this reason had come to visualize the father complex also as something separate. Yet it is difficult to understand how Freud's relation to Breuer could play no essential role in such a personal volume as the *Interpretation*, in contrast to the banal event of a mature man losing his father whom he had spiritually long since outgrown. In fact, one may scarcely doubt which event in the life of the forty-year-old Freud was the more important: the death of his father, or his simultaneous separation from Breuer, whom he had to thank for the key to his understanding of the neurotic, and from whom he was compelled to separate in order to pursue his own development.

I shall appeal here only to generally known facts and not go deeply into Freud's biography, since I am trying to give an analysis not of Freud, but only of his psychology and of psychology in general as an essentially projective affair, and as an individual's attempt to create his own comfort and consolation. A detailed proof that most of Freud's dreams prior to the *Interpretation of Dreams* really concerned Breuer, or that they were influenced by him, would lead us too far from our theme and too deep into Freud's purely personal affairs. Moreover, I believe that every reader can use this key to the problem because the relationships are apparent even without Freud's ever having said a word about them. There is only the information that Freud counted his relation with Breuer among those permissible "discretions" which he acknowledged in his "foreword" to the first edition. But this was not very probable, because the fact of his separation from Breuer was known, and because Freud exposed a degree of intimacy inconsistent with his acknowledgment of feelings toward an old colleague that were not entirely friendly. One must either assume that Freud's dreams which stemmed from the period of his separation conflict had no role in the matter, or grant my assertion that this separation played so important a role that Freud had to deny it and substitute for it his more banal relation to his father.

Freud's separation from Breuer, which really corresponded to his departure from earlier, purely medical ideals, appears to have come about gradually around 1895, with the complete break in their personal relations coming later.[28] This "death" or "killing" of Breuer was a *loss* the reaction to which the rationalized *Interpretation of Dreams* displaced onto the con-

[28] It would not even be unlikely that the death of Freud's father in 1896 had hastened or even effected his final step toward independence.

current death of Freud's father. For the moment, let us neglect the motive for this displacement, and consider the consequences which such a denial of actuality and displacement into the past must have had for Freud's theorizing. Once this displacement was introduced and Breuer had been replaced by Freud's father, whose death was identified with Freud's loss of Breuer, a motive had to be found in Freud's childhood for Freud's ostensible death wish against his father, which Freud's dream seemed to imply. This motive appeared in the fable of Oedipus, which was then built into the core both of Freud's interpretation of dreams and into the psychology he built on this interpretation. The Oedipus material also allowed the death wish against the father to unite with the desire to possess the mother sexually, and so enabled Freud to postulate the sex drive as the cause of ambitious desires.

Before we pursue other implications of this view we must return to the question what should cause such a displacement from actuality to the past, both in Freud's case and in general. The answer I have is a simple one: such displacement has a therapeutic effect in the broadest sense of the word, and illustrates a wholly generalized process in mental life. Freud himself has shown that an individual's various conflicts are mutually related, and it is just these relationships which make the therapeutic effect possible. If the "guilt-father" (*pater peccavi*) can be displaced from the present into the past, there can be a momentary discharge of guilt feeling and an attitude of consolation and forgiveness. For Freud, the connection between actuality and the past existed for the guilt problem as well, and this connection was established in Freud's relation to Breuer as in his relation to his father without being "transferred" to Breuer. But the *Interpretation of Dreams* does not show a single attempt on Freud's part to want to understand and explain his relation to Breuer on the basis of his father complex, as one would expect him to do in the light of his theory; rather are Breuer and his relation to Freud absolutely nonexistent either as problems or memories. This is a complete denial which was ultimately covered up completely by the father problem. I say "denial" because psychologically it is absolutely impossible that Freud's recent memory of his painful conflict with Breuer and of their decisive separation could have become as completely erased as it would seem to have been in the *Interpretation of Dreams*.

As I have mentioned before, this cannot be a matter of discretion on Freud's part, because he expanded it into a vital feature of the whole book. As I know, none of the citations of persons by initial letters which appear in the *Interpretation of Dreams* referred to Breuer; on the other hand, important roles were played by "Friend O.," a colleague to whom Freud bore obligations, and by "Friend P.," a rival colleague. But Freud was obviously blind to Breuer's point of view. So, when he wondered apropos of the "uncle dream" that he could recall only the name Joseph, of his fifth uncle (see the note on page 96 of the first edition), or the dream *non vixit* (241 ff) which betrays Breuer's "killing" most clearly (Freud turned it into *non vivit*), he was brought back to Kaiser Joseph Street. Freud himself observed the frequent appearance of the name Joseph in the *Interpretation of Dreams*, but explained it by its identification with Pharaoh's dream interpreter, and not in relation to the fact that he had put himself in the place of his friend Joseph Breuer.[29]

[29] I suppose that Freud's interest in forgetting, following his separation from Breuer and during his occupation with the *Interpretation of Dreams*, was connected with the displacement of Breuer from his memory. In the first example (1898), in Freud's *Psychopathology of everyday life* (Psychopathologie des Alltagslebens), Freud was unable to recall the name of

Regarding Freud's denial of Breuer, perhaps one would not exaggerate in saying that the entire *Interpretation of Dreams* tends to prove the nonexistence of Breuer and to leave Freud's far less painful father alive. For the appearance of Freud's late father in one of his dreams is not only understandable as a displacement of Breuer, but, according to ancient spiritual belief, it evidences the immortality of the soul in general and of Freud's own self in particular. After Breuer's "killing" and the death of Freud's father, it was as though Freud needed this dream to insure his own immortality. And, finally, one may recognize a third motive which probably implies an anxiety dream: namely, the basis for Freud's unsuccessful attempt to put the living Breuer out of the way. Here we encounter again an important principle of the psychological interpretation of spiritual dream content. Freud investigated the dreams in which his father appeared, only with regard to his own attitude toward his father, and neglected to interpret the father himself. In other settings Freud knew quite well that a dream may frequently substitute one person for another, and he often made full use of the significance of so-called "mixed persons." But when his father appeared in one of his dreams he was taken at face value, just as Freud made a similar exception in his attitude toward his dream of sexual intercourse with his mother. Had Freud been at all free to do so, he would have sensed that this ancient spiritual motive was utterly opposed to his psychological interpretation. But had he excluded his father from the interpretive role, Breuer would have appeared in most of his dreams. For this

the Italian painter Signorelli, and obtained instead two substitutes, each of which began with the letter B. ("Sigm." is the abbreviation Freud used for his given name.) False recollection appeared concerning a traveler whom Freud accompanied on part of a journey, and, as Freud confessed, this recollection was concerned with compulsive thoughts of death.

reason Freud was obliged to discover in his unconscious the latent displacement emotions of resistance against his father— all the while his own attitude lay within his own self, and not in the intellectual content of his manifest dream! In other words, when one actually puts Breuer instead of Freud's father into those dreams that refer to him, one may safely discount the hero's misrepresentation of his attitude and ascribe meaning to much of the manifest account of the dream.

In both a theoretical and therapeutic sense, we see here the birth of psychology from self-illusion. We say "theoretical," because the entire complicated associative and interpretive methodology, and even the creation of the dream itself, become possible and necessary only through a misunderstanding of the true facts of the case; and we say "therapeutic," because the unburdening displacement of affect from actuality to the past had to be justified in theory. For from therapeutic displacement, which operates only to unburden when it does not concern the right person, and is then psychologically false, Freud derived a general law of psychic causality which should allow for displacement backwards along the associative links. This was possible only because Freud excluded a certain direction of displacement from the general tendency to unburden: namely, the specific displacement of reality into the past, which Freud proclaimed as a principle of causal explanation. But even in the doctrine of regression, where Freud emphasized this special direction of displacement into the past, he excepts particular items on the basis of the same *petitio principii* which he had designated as the "causes" accountable for therapeutic displacement. Otherwise one cannot understand why recall of actual conflict with the father was not just as good a regression (consoling displacement of reality into the past) as it was a displacement in another direction, which masked itself as a return along the chain of causation.[30]

The Freudian *Interpretation of Dreams* is shown to be a therapeutic effort in the grand style which serves, however, not to improve reality in the sense of wish fulfillment, but to ratify the alteration, misrepresentation, and denial of reality by dreams and their interpretation. For Freud, Breuer was dead though alive. Therefore Breuer did not appear in his dream, and could not be recognized in its interpretation. Freud used his dream therapeutically, or as a consolation for his self-knowledge, because he excluded from it and thus "killed" the one he wished were dead (Breuer); and in Breuer's place there appeared only the deceased father who had not been killed.[30a]

Just as the appearance of another person in a dream was a proof of immortality at the spiritual stage of history, his failure to appear was now a proof of death. Freud wanted to show that it was not the soul of the dead which appeared in dreams, as superstition claimed, but one's own soul manifested in the form of psychology (wishes). But psychology would only amount to a recognition of Breuer's significance instead of its denial. If so, then perhaps the entire *Interpretation of Dreams* was unnecessary, as well as that broader (psychological) interpretation which had to call again upon ancient spiritual belief (dead father) for help. But like an-

[30] Actually, this possibility has been granted even by one of Freud's followers on the basis of my critique in *The Trauma of Birth* (Trauma der Geburt); see, for example, F. Alexander, *Internat. Zeitschr. f. psa.*, XI, 1925, 173 f.

[30a] Similarly there appears to Macbeth not the ghost of Duncan whom he himself had killed, but only the ghost of Banquo whom he had ordered killed.

cient spiritual belief, this was therapy and not psychology. Therefore, wish fulfillment in the *Interpretation of Dreams* lay in the dream's interpretation rather than in its content, whereas in the spiritual era such fulfillment lay in the dream apart from its content. In the present psychological era the dream is no longer transmuted into reality; instead, reality is transposed and confirmed by the dream. This explains both the complete inversion of the primitive method of interpretation, which created experience from a dream accepted as true, and the corresponding rise of psychological interpretation, which explains an illusory dream content on the basis of already justified experience. The realistic ideology of the psychological era corresponds to this view, as the animistic ideology of the spiritual era did to the other. But, as already noted, there is no one meaning and interpretation of the dream which is good for all time; the spiritual phenomenon of the dream is rather interpreted according to the currently ruling ideology which was once animistic, then sexual, and is now psychological. But interpretation always tends to maintain and confirm the ancient spiritual belief, in spite of all accommodations of its meaning to any new ideology.

Originally the dream was only a proof of spiritual belief in both positive and negative senses (wish and anxiety dream), because it exhibited not only one's own body-soul but the souls of others (deceased) whom now one wished to be dead. During the sexual era, the dream served to alter reality in the sense of spiritual belief, or to concretize it in order to make it true and to prove the existence of the soul. Finally, in the psychological era, the dream is interpreted according to a realistic ideology in order to salvage a dwindling spiritual belief from the content of the dream. Yet one can understand these distinctions only if one remembers that

137

dream content itself changes according to the currently ruling ideology; in the development of the individual, simple wish dreams and anxiety dreams become supplanted by fantasy and ideational dreams that correspond to the realistic ideology of the psychological era, just as childish dreams correspond to the animistic or sexual era. The simple wish dreams of the animistic stage signified reality; the anxiety dreams of the sexual era, in which the individual protected himself against procreative mortality, connoted the future in the sense of translation of spiritual belief into action; and the fantasy and ideational dreams of the psychological stage are explained by the past, to which there corresponds only the consolation that the ancient soul survives in the dream without any causal explanation of the phenomenon of the dream itself.[30b] But this final interpretation of the dream content also fails to explain the dream because the tendency toward wish fulfillment is characteristic not only of dreams but of spiritual or mental affairs in general, and because this tendency inheres in all its manifestations, including spiritual belief.

As already noted, the unique characteristic of the dream is sleep. Aristotle had already established this point for the purpose of his physiological explanation of dreams in relation to sleep. But, as the dream shows us, sleep is not just a physical phenomenon which makes the dream possible. There is also a psychological set or attitude of the sleeper toward his own sleeping body, which seems to me to constitute the essence of the dream. This is not just an attitude of the dreamer toward his sleeping body in general, but toward

[30b] I find the correction in Werner Achelis' (Stuttgart, 1928) "philosophical dissertation" (philosophischen Abhandlung) on "the problem of the dream" (das Problem des Traumes), in which he advocates a proposition based on Schopenhauer's world view: "All dreams are true dreams."

sleep as a deathlike state, and toward his powerless and prostrate body as one that has "slept away" (died). This attitude changes according to the kind and depth of the sleep and to the psychic mood of the dreamer, but it always retains a tendency to deny the similarity of the sleeping condition to death and to assure the sleeping self that it is still alive. I believe now that dreaming is derived from the tendency to frighten away the death anxiety which sleep produces, by assuring the sleeper that he still lives. In the dream this is mediated by thinking, feeling, and seeing, and especially by certain sensory and bodily organs activated, as in myth, by eating or other functions which I have accordingly designated before as "awakening symptoms." The dreamer's interpretation of his sleeping self turns out, then, according to his mood and to the depth of his sleep. Primitively, he can insure his hunger or thirst in an hallucinatory fashion because such matters do not concern actual bodily needs, but only assure his existence, which dream thirst and dream water cannot do. The same also holds for many patently sexual dreams which symbolize life even according to psychoanalysis, and it certainly holds for the dream itself as a proof of the bodily soul. With the body-soul, man took his first significant step into a supernatural world, because it assured him not only that he still lived while he slept, but that he could sleep peacefully without dying.

However, this disclosed the negative side of spiritual belief, because the appearance of other body-souls (including those of the deceased) could not always be reconciled with man's general immortality theory, and because this appearance was often regarded as evidence of man's own mortal nature. In other words, according to bodily (sleep) and psychic (moods) premises, not only the condition of sleep itself but that of one's own appearance in a dream could be interpreted as reminders of death, which compelled the sleeper to awaken and thereby reëstablish the fact of his existence. As the condition of sleep itslf shows, there are certain dreams whose feeling tone depends more on bodily states, and others whose feeling tone depends on the psychic mood which interprets the state of sleep. Dreams with strong bodily sensations, such as those of flying or falling, may depend on the condition of the sleeping body (heavy or light), but at the spiritual stage they are interpreted as immortality (flying) or mortality (falling), and at the psychological stage as wish-dreams or anxiety-dreams. Even when actual bodily stimuli are involved (as in hunger, thirst, sex, etc.), these dreams can always be interpreted as evidence of life in the sense of spiritual ideology, although the current mood (death anxiety) just as often made them conscious evidence of life. As may be readily seen, this view makes it possible to reconcile the various theories of dreams, including those which refer to bodily and psychic stimuli, and also various interpretive methods such as the spiritual, the sexual, the psychological, and that one designated by H. Silberer as "functional,"[31] which sees dreams as figurative (symbolic) representations of spiritual functions.

But the dream itself is an interpretive phenomenon, because the sleeping self is compelled to interpret all bodily and psychic stimuli according to spiritual belief. This interpretation is the dream. Proof that the self is not dead is

---

[31] The work of the author referred to, who died in 1923, appears in the *Jahrbuch für psychoanalytische Forschungen* (Yearbook for Psychoanalytic Research), 1909-1912, and in the *Zentralblatt für Psychoanalyse* (Central Journal of Psychoanalysis), 1911-1914. *The Psychology of Daydreams* by the Belgian psychologist, J. Varendonck (who died in 1924), concerns the same area of problem.

granted the individual in every instance, be it through the dreaming itself, which activates certain functions, through that special form of the dream which displays the soul as independent of the body and therefore immortal, or through awakening from a threatening anxiety dream which proves the real existence of the self. Other items appearing in the dream content are the active thought remnants and sensations of waking life, which appear when the sleeper partially awakens in order to prove that he is still alive, and are significant for the dream only to the extent to which they affect their own interpretation by the dreamer or are evoked from him for the purpose of an interpretation. However, a causal *explanation* of the dream is not possible, principally because the dream can only be further *interpreted*, so that we have interpretations, supplementary interpretations, and supra-interpretations without end.

Psychoanalysis did not explain the dream, but only derived a psychology from it. Because this psychology interpreted the dream scientifically as a spiritual phenomenon, it was doomed both to fail as a theory and to indicate only a tendency to wish fulfillment. As a scientific psychology, psychoanalysis denied the soul and misplaced the gratification of wishes onto the content of the dream, instead of leaving it with the dream itself where it belonged. But as a depth psychology, psychoanalysis could not really dispense with spirituality, for Freud used his own spiritual experience (his father's death) and a psychological ideology to explain those dreams that arose from his psychic experience (Breuer). Whereas man once tried to use spiritual belief to confirm his spiritual self, he now tries to use this new psychology to preserve only his psychic individuality.

SOUL AND WILL

> *Divinity, joined to thy will,*
> *Rises from its earthly throne.*
>
> SCHILLER

THE PRIMITIVE IDENTIFICATION OF dream and reality, and the willed translation of dream into action, which survive even in our modern point of view, bring us to *willing*, which is the psychological problem *par excellence*. As in my will psychology and will therapy,[1] I substitute this problem for the narcissistic one of the wish. It was the will to live, and not death anxiety, which produced belief in immortality, and it is the will which creates the dream. The dream seems to prove freedom of will to us as completely as it did to primitive man who translated his dream into reality. While the soul and body had originally been united in one being, primitive man began to interpret this freedom of the will as freedom of the soul from the body. But in his dream life his own soul's freedom of will was opposed by that of other souls which seemed to appear

---

[1] *Truth and Reality; Sketch of a Spiritual Philosophy* (Wahrheit und Wirklichkeit; Entwurf einer Philosophie des Seelischen), 1929; and *The Analytic Reaction in its Constructive Aspects* (Die analytische Reaktion in ihren konstruktiven Elementen), 1929. Both published by F. Deuticke Press, Vienna and Leipzig.

in his dream as uninvited visitors. Early metaphysicists explained the dream on the basis of a temporary withdrawal of the will during sleep. Freud, who regarded willing as the driving power of the dream, denied this freedom because he needed neither the soul nor willing to demonstrate the causal determination of psychic events. But the will problem cannot be solved by the dream or by any particular spiritual phenomenon, since it represents a phenomenon already affected by spiritual belief and interpreted in relation to it. Spiritual belief itself proves to be an expression of the will to live.

The single real obstacle which freedom of will encounters is death, which it conquers by spiritual belief. Though it may seem curious, this victory of will over death appears to have been portrayed by primitive man's actual behavior. In the traditions of the Traveler, Faster, etc., which were cited in the preceding chapter, the hero's attainment of immortality was independent of others' death which the water spirit had promised him. It seems almost as if primitive man died in order not to get killed. Again, this does not signify self-preservation, but a "causal" proof that the individual will is god even over death which it can cause. Evidence of one's own power of will in the struggle with death appears also in suicide, which is possible and understandable only as a victory of will over death. Primitive man could comprehend only a "willed" death resulting from his transgression of a tabu, a phenomenon which we encounter at the psychological stage in the form of a wish to die, which Freud interpreted biologically as a "death instinct." But this wish to die represents only a will victory for the individual who creates a voluntary affirmation out of uncompromising necessity. Although death formerly appeared as a result of one's own

143

mistakes, it was subsequently brought about by one's own desire, and at no time was it a fate thrust upon the individual, but a destiny which the individual took it upon himself to effect.

Up to this point we have been considering principally the emergence of the idea of fear and death from spiritual belief. We turn now to the positive side of spirituality, which primitives regarded as an expression of life power. "Tanuá," the word for the soul, also means life-power and shadows among the aborigines of New Mecklenburg,[2] and thus connotes life as well as death. Most primitives express these two ideas by different spiritual symbols. In the Salomo Islands off the coast of Florida, the soul was called "tarunga," or life-power, as long as it dwelt in the body; but after death when it had assumed the form of its former bodily host it was called "tindal," or spirit-being.

> On Maewo, (Aurora) the northernmost island of the New Hebrides, the incarnate soul was called "tamani," or life-spirit (from "ata" or spirit, and "mani" or life); when separated from the body, and in its own proper form, it was called "tamate" or death-spirit. On Efata the soul which dwelt in the human body was called "atamauri" (from "ata" or spirit, and "mauri" or life), but when it became free to assume its own form it became "atamate" (from "ata," or spirit, and "mate" meaning death or the dead). (From Cunow, p. 35.)

Corresponding differentiations among spiritual concepts are to be found among the Polynesian and Micronesian peoples of the South Seas. These are not only related to the

[2] According to Heinrich Cunow: *Origin of Religion and Belief in God* (Ursprung der Religion und des Gottesglaubens), Berlin, 1923.

two souls of the North American Indians mentioned above, but to the dual meaning of the soul concept itself in relation to life (power) and death (anxiety).

In order to understand this positive and creative meaning of spirituality we may recall that ethnologists assume a pre-animistic stage of "emanism" to have been the oldest in human culture. The idea basic to emanism was that of "mana," as the Melanesians termed that supernatural power which almost all peoples know under one name or another (the "Orenda" of the Iroquois, "Wakanda" of the Sioux, "Tjurunga" of the Australians, "Brahma" of the Hindus, etc.). Ethnologists have found it quite hard to clarify the idea of "mana," although primitive man appeared to be quite clear about it in spite of the supernatural characteristics which he ascribed to it. From an extensive literature I may cite a few characteristics of this concept in order to show the degree to which carefully defined views of primitives cover what I have designated psychologically as will.[3]

Thus the missionary bishop Codrington (*The Melanesians*, 1891), who was one of the most thorough scholars of the Samoan Archipelago, says:

> There is a belief in a power which is entirely different from natural power, which effects good and evil in all possible ways and which it is to one's greatest advantage to possess or control. That is "mana." . . . It is unnatural but in a certain sense supernatural power or influence; yet it manifests itself in natural forces and in any kind of power or superiority which the individual human

[3] See particularly the outstanding presentation by Karl Bethe: *Religion and Magic. A Contribution by History of Religion to the Psychological Foundations of Religious Dogma.* (Religion und Magie. Ein religionsgeschichtlicher Beitrag zur psychologischen Grundlegung der religiösen Prinzipienlehre), second edition, Leipzig, 1927.

may possess. . . . As far as religious customs, offerings, and sacrifices go, all Melanesian religion amounts to obtaining this mana for oneself, or to being allowed to use it for one's needs. . . . This mana is not tied to any particular thing, and it can be applied anywhere. Spirits, souls separated from bodies, and supernatural beings possess it, and can impart it.

Though conceived impersonally, this power is "always bound to some person who controls it," and one expects him who is gifted with the power to achieve unusual things. Humans who have it and whom we currently call "strong personalities," use it to rise to power over others, as shamans, priests, doctors, and kings. Every manifest accomplishment of a person evidences his possession of mana.

There is no doubt that in all its aspects this power corresponds to the human will, which is the creative personality I have described particularly as a power standing outside and over natural causality. For, according to Codrington's further description of this concept, which comes to us as it were out of a clear sky, mana is "that invisible power which the aborigines believe causes all effects transcending the usual course of natural events." It is "the active power in everything they do, and which they believe occurs in white or black magic. By means of it humans are in a position to govern and control nature," and to use it "to their own advantage" (Codrington, *op. cit.*, p. 118, footnote). Tregear, the lexicographer of Polynesian dialects, frankly defines mana as psychic energy; Hubert and Mauss essentially refer every expression of power to it, and the *Encyclopedia Britannica* defines it as "magical power invested in individuals whose wills rule the universe."

However, primitive conceptions of mana not only recog-

146

nize but also try to explain this particularly personal will power in individuals. This first animistic explanation of the will problem which we have regarded as an early step towards psychology was spiritual and not psychological. It underlay the Platonic world-soul, the Hellenistic doctrine of pneuma, Schelling's romantic nature-soul, Aristotle's doctrine of body and soul, Leibnitz's doctrine of the monad, and modern vitalism. In animism we have seen how everything supernatural was derived from the spiritual interpretation of the will as a psychic phenomenon because, as something invisible and ineffable, the will defied causal comprehension. The origin and effect of will expressions were incalculable, and will power itself was incomprehensible and therefore unnatural. But even the magical transference of will power, which we currently call suggestion without understanding it any better than did primitive man, is in itself puzzling enough, and certainly seems supernatural. Therefore it is not to be wondered that this mysterious power was considered as the "cause" of such an inexplicable and important fact as death. Since the belief that anyone could die a natural death was foreign to primitives,[4] death was regarded as being effected by another person's mana, and since this other person could be either dead or alive, this view led forthwith to a belief in demons. However, we recognize in these propositions a fact important for the treatment of our next chapter: that because of their causal incomprehensibility, just these simple human phenomena of will and death were regarded as supernatural. They were related to natural forces only at a much later period, not

[4] Spencer and Gillen: *The Primitives of Central Australia*, p. 476. Karl von den Steinen, in his *With the Primitives of Central Brazil* (Unter den Naturvölkern Zentralbrasiliens), says of the Bakairi that they do not recognize the necessity of death, and generally know no "musts."

147

because they were derived from such forces, but because these forces made them more comprehensible.

In this connection it is important to note that although mana was to be found in every unusual object of nature and human life, it was not bound up with any idea of a higher divine or spiritual being, but was rather a concept of power. At this period the being most highly gifted with mana was just the strong-willed human who interfered with the course of natural events and determined the fate of other humans. It was only gradually that this psychological will concept came to be allied with the soul, and with the godhead which at a later period came to represent the soul. This evolution, which began with the first animistic will theory, is one which we would like principally to pursue for the moment. Corresponding to the two souls, or to the dualistic view of the soul concept, there are two roots of religion which have never really grown together even in highly monotheistic systems. These roots are: the idea of God, and belief in immortality. In following the development of immortality belief from the individual body-soul to a belief in collective rebirth, we have differentiated spiritual rebirth of the animistic era from bodily rebirth in the sexual era, of which elements Christianity appears to have achieved a sublime synthesis. However, the concept of God as a higher Being equipped with supernatural power was developed not from death anxiety, but from the wish to live, whose energetic power was expressed in the concept of mana. In other words, God was a personification of the individual will-ego, and was felt to be immortal, both because he possessed mana, and because the soul corresponded to a collective immortality whose ego had to be protected from the threat of death. Thus the soul was the general

148

mana of all, or the folk-mana which the community acquired by levies upon personalities gifted with mana, and which to some degree religion made available to all. Hence the primitive rule that the bearer of mana must use his power not to his own advantage, but to that of the commonwealth or tribe (to which, for example, the fathers in the Traveler and Faster stood opposed).

At a very much earlier stage the concept of the soul appeared allied with mana or life power, and as the cited linguistic relationships show, the immortal soul was originally identified with mana. In totemistic systems this surviving individual soul was united with the collective soul or generic totem, which finally evolved into the idea of God. This spirit-god already represented collective immortality, and for that reason all individuals were obliged to believe in him lest they lose his favor. Contemporary with this spirit-god, if not with his earlier prototypes, there was the will-god who personified not the collective soul or immortality, but an augmented mana or individual survival. For what mana made so clear, particularly in its magic practices, was the belief that this supernatural power could even protect and preserve life or cause death. This explains the now established "fact that one finds in a remarkably large number of lower cultures a belief in an exalted heavenly deity" (Bethe, p. 332) which, over and above all possible forms of spiritual belief, "appears as an autochthonous religious concept."[5] For,

[5] In *The Origin of the Idea of God* (Der Ursprung der Gottesidee, Munster, formerly two volumes), W. Schmidt has developed from this point the hypothesis of a primal monotheism. The merit of the contribution by Taylor, who first comprehended and formulated animism from an anthropological point of view, is considerably reduced by two defects in this theory which, on the one hand, conceives of the animistic soul too rationalistically and causally, and, on the other, confuses it with the religious concept of God. A. Lang, in *The Making of Religion,* has corrected this

as is the case among a few African tribes (*loc. cit.*, p. 349) or among Australian aborigines, it represents certainly not the souls of the dead, but a magnified superman who never dies. This appears to be borne out by Strehlow's[6] demonstration that in the Arandas' language (Old Jirerama) the word for dream means "god-seeing." Although Strehlow adds that it is not the highest god in Heaven but a totem god which the aborigine believes he sees in his dream, it seems to me that this does not prove the identity of this heavenly deity with the aborigine's ancestors. For what appears in the dream is certainly the true will-ego which the Australian aborigine interprets so as to vindicate his totemistic ideology, just as we use it to justify the natural science ideology of our psychological era.

Egyptologists have recently been inclined to agree with theologists that real religion begins beyond emanism, animism, totemism, and even beyond primitive monotheism in which God merely represented an exalted self. I believe, however, that decisive criteria for the beginning of the religious era can be established only through psychological understanding, and not on the basis of voluminous ethnological facts or theological dogma. Such understanding is possible only by a return to such fundamental psychic phenomena as the will, and it cannot be achieved by psychoanalysis' causal reduction of religion to reality, which itself corresponds to an earlier interpretation of psychic facts. For

error by his penetrating reference to two different factors in the formation of religion. (Compare with this theme the basic presentation by J. Pascher: *The Concept of the Soul in Taylor's "Animism"* (Der Seelenbegriff in Animismus Taylors), Würzburg, 1929.)

[6] *The Aranda and Loritja tribes in Central Australia* (Die Aranda- und Loritja-Stämme in Zentralaustralien). See also Spencer and Gillen: *The Arunta*, London, 1927.

emanism, and animism which is based on emanism, were spiritual attempts to explain the will problem in the sense of belief in individual immortality, just as totemism corresponded to a concretion of animism in the sense of procreative rebirth. All these spiritual theories about psychic and biological facts were used as materials with which to create religion. This creation did not consist of a mere fusion of theory into a simple capacity to resign oneself and believe, as happened with the will- and soul-gods. Rather is real religion characterized by a certain new attitude toward these spiritually interpreted human facts, and this attitude can be explained only through psychological understanding.

From a pure ego psychology, which for myself had finally crystallized into willing as the crucial personality problem, I have been led to a will-god without considering ethnological materials or theological points of view at all.[6a] Yet I can understand this elevation of the ego religiously only to the extent of its alliance with negative will or with self-resignation and humiliation. The new attitude which manifested itself as "religious" was that which came to use such prereligious spiritual creations as the will-god to justify individual willing. *Only with this moral tendency to justify does naïve projection of life power into spiritual immortality*

[6a] See in *Truth and Reality* (Wahrheit und Wirklichkeit), especially the chapter "Creation and guilt" (Schaffen und Schuld).—The general notion of the creation of God in man's image was apparently expressed first by Aristotle: "Man forms the external features and the living relations between his gods according to his own image" (Politics, I, 7). In his *Natural History of Religion*, Hume subsequently developed the thought that the pressures of social living, and not those of natural influences, determine man's religious ideas. Finally, Ludwig Feuerbach psychologized this religious anthropology, because he explained God in terms of the divine likeness of man, and considered gods as the creations of human wishes and needs. See *The Nature of Christianity* (Das Wesen des Christentums), 1841.

151

acquire that ethical stamp which we associate with religion.
Yet how did it happen that, under pressure of moral compulsion, the individual's compulsion to justify himself and
his willing changed from a positive force of self-affirmation
and action into a negative attitude of self-disparagement and
subjugation? Timid reverence before supernatural and other-
worldly events was not the primary attitude of natural man,
who was much more concerned with his own problems than
with those of nature and the universe. Reverent humility
before exalted beings was just a result of this reëvaluation
of will, from which arose the concepts of guilt and sin.

We should like to try to understand spiritually this ancient and fundamental problem of religion, this moral attitude toward the will and its interpretation as evil, which we
encounter in the concepts of guilt and sin as personal offenses. In the later traditions of the sexual era, which regard
woman as the chief evil and sexuality as the "cause" of mortality, we discover only ancient spiritual belief recast into
the new ideology of procreative immortality. That is to say,
the curse of sexuality follows from its destruction of man's
belief in individual immortality. We may also recall that, as
long as its necessity was denied, natural death, which was
the first evil known to man, was believed to follow from his
own trangressions. Primitive traditions have given us much
information concerning these transgressions, which always
aimed essentially at winning individual immortality but were
always punished by death.

The conflict between the individual mortal soul and the
collective immortal soul originating from the life strength
of mana continued in the religious personifications of the
will-god and soul-god. The reëvaluation of will which produced real religion had already been introduced by the indi-

152

vidual's cession of mana to society, or of the power of a living soul to the souls of the dead which, as demons, became even more powerful than the living bearer of mana. Thus fear of the denied necessity of dying first entered primitive consciousness as a fear of the dead, rather than of death itself. For with the few exceptions of the nearest relatives, the dead used their mana primarily to kill or capture the living in order to restore themselves through the latters' life force. Herein lay the origin of spirit and ancestral cults, as Australian negroid culture so well exemplifies.[7] The living presented even blood-offerings to their dead ancestors and sought to restrain their dead enemies, in order that they could retain their life power for themselves. The sacrifices which serve essentially to protect the one making them amount more or less to surrendering one's individuality to the community, but in this case to the community of the dead, whose demands upon primitive man were more imperative than were those which elicited his complete and automatic surrender to the community of the living. The dead comprised an immanent threat to vital existence, and to the continuing spiritual existence which society quite straightforwardly guaranteed.

This fear of the dead, which led to a voluntary relinquishment of mana or to a self-restriction of will, became religious self-subjugation by a process described spiritually as a progressive fusion of will-god with soul-god. This prereligious evolution is paralleled by the animistic replacement of belief in individual immortality by a collective spiritual belief. Only with the will- and the soul-god, man had already gone back to the preanimistic ego stage, because he was again personifying the collective will as he had the collective soul,

[7] See especially, A. W. Howitt: *Native Tribes of Southeast Australia.*

153

namely, as images of single individuals and of their individual wills and souls. Meanwhile collectivistic ideology of immortality had become so much more powerful than naïve immortality of the self, that the attempt to perpetuate the originally mana-laden will-man as a combined will- and soul-god had to fail. Instead, the individual will-god became absorbed by the collective will-god, just as the individual soul had previously been captured by the totem soul, and the individual by society.

Spiritual fear of the dead now became fear of the new god who represented spiritual belief and mana belief as individual and collective immortality. For this deity's will power was so weakened by concessions to the all-spiritual, and his stamina so undermined by the continuing claims of individuals, that he could support belief neither in personal nor communal immortality. He became a Janus-faced symbol of that raging conflict between the individual's two souls which leads to the knowledge and recognition of death. Death, the original and sole evil in the world, could no longer be denied. Its inevitability, which was not yet conceded, was interpreted morally and not spiritually. Denied, death again emerged as an evil, now no longer projected on the evil spirits of the dead, demons, evil-wishing mana bearers or sorcerers, but interpreted as a moralistic concept of guilt and sin, and damned for what it was in relation to man. In other words, at this religious stage neither the wish for immortality nor that for sexuality was the cause of death; it was the *will* which demanded even the death that was the root of all evil. At the same time the damnation of will became transferred to the new god, who then punished as well as "rewarded." But man's submission to this godhead was only a submission to the power of death, which recog-

154

nized the moralistic form of self-abasement and the vanity
of human existence. We can discern here the moralistic
formulation of the original immortality ideology, to the effect
that man was the cause of his own death because death was
otherwise impossible. But the godhead which could now kill
was that same will which had once guaranteed man eternal
life and immortality, a will now weakened and broken by
the knowledge of death's inevitability.

The most outstanding type of this religiously revalued
will-god was the Hebrews' Jahweh who in other respects
was purely monotheistic in character. However, this monotheism was a maturing rather than a primitive one, and it
was a synthesis of various prereligious conceptions into a
religious godhead whose essence lay in just the unification
of the soul-, will-, and death-gods into one entity. This deity
manifested traits of the earthly mana bearers whose will[8]
could effect good or evil, and the corresponding Double-
trait of the beneficent or malignant souls of the dead. He
was a typical incarnation of will justification and a personification of moral principle itself. Modern critics of the Bible
have traced his apparent unity back to three different sources
which may be brought into harmony with the three prereligious belief forms which we have already considered. A
recent incisive study based on Bachofen's views makes it
likely that the Jahwehistic literary sources were colored by
the preceding matriarchial culture in contrast with the lit-

[8] The Elohim-concept of the Pentateuch is not a symbol of good, but of
power which was used on things as well as man. See Goldberg's: *The
Reality of the Hebrews* (Die Wirklichkeit der Hebräer), Berlin, 1925,
105 f. I believe, moreover, that the dual sense of the Word, or "Verba,"
as found in Hebraic and other primitive languages, expresses the polarity
of the will, or a simultaneous positive and negative willing. Armin Blau
gives an example of this in his work: *On the Dual Meaning of the Word
in the Hebraic* (Ueber den Gegensinn der Worte im Hebräischen).

erature of the priesthood in which patriarchy was dominant. "Matriarchy and patriarchy compete in original biblical history, with the tendency toward final conquest of matriarchy predominating. In the story of Genesis the priesthood celebrates the victory of the paternal light principle."[9]

We can understand Israelitic henotheism which bears the seed of monotheism only if we remember that the struggle of emerging patriarchy against matriarchy belonged to the sexual era, and not to that of spiritual belief of which nothing at all appears in the Old Testament. The feminine character Heva, whose name Gunkel relates to the Phoenician serpent goddess of the lower world, was not only the mother of all living things, but the mortal representative of the ancient earth mother, and the death goddess of the lower world from whom mankind sprang and to whom it returned. Eve's husband originally had no name; as earth symbol, Eve herself was that *adama* (moist earth) "from which Adam *homo ex homo* was formed. Adam must return to *adama:* 'for from her wert thou taken' (3, 19)" (*op. cit.*, p. 65). Hence Cain killed not his father who was anonymous, but his brother. I regard Cain's fratricide as further evidence of the recasting of the old spiritual belief into the ideology of the sexual era, for at this stage Abel was only Cain's concretized Double or twin brother, in whom the second soul of the individual was personified as it had been in a mythological era. In this entire biblical tradition, which was oriented to the present, Cain represented the first man born of woman to lose the spiritual immortality which Abel embodied, who murdered the soul, and therefore became mortal. The objec-

[9] Wilhelm Vischer: *Jahweh, the God of Cain* (Jahwe der Gott Kains), Munich, 1929, p. 67. Various investigators have already referred to the matriarchal characteristics of Jahwehistic literary sources. *Cf.* H. Gunkel: "Genesis," fifth chapter, p. 42, where reference is made to further literature.

tion to the effect that Abel actually died, while Cain whom the matriarchial godhead, Jahweh, deprived of blood vengeance survived,[10] is covered by the ideological evolution inherent in the transition from the spiritual to the sexual era. "The name of the immortal spiritual Double who became mortal during this transition was 'häbäl,' which was the biblical term for inconsolable emptiness and the frailty of human existence: *ak kol häbäl kol adam*—every Adam is an Abel. The name Abel symbolized the bitter knowledge that outside of paradise there is no life that is not also death" (*loc. cit.*, 42).

God acquired fatherly traits only in the sexual era, because an earthly father then possessed the "divine" capacity to produce children. In the sources of the Elohists of the arch-father-god this newly accepted capacity is reiterated *ad nauseam*. In the father god the personal father was depicted not as an ancestor but as a type, that is, as man of the sexual era who had exchanged the new ideology for the old—and not, as Freud meant, one who became an exalted physical father following his death by his own default, but one who in the course of history has become the type exalted in the father, the confessor of sexual ideology. Thus at this stage we can understand how the will-god became the world creator described by the patriarchial Elohist of Genesis. In other cultures of the sexual era this process went along with the cleavage of the godhead into its original components, the gods of the higher and lower worlds in whom the paternal and maternal principles were again separated as in the immortal and mortal souls. In the Christian

---

[10] Vischer agrees to Stade's thesis that Jahweh deprived Cain of blood vengeance (by the sign of Cain) which he incurred by his murder. See B. Stade's "The sign of Cain" (Das Kainzeichen), Z A W, XIV, 1894, 250 ff.

PSYCHOLOGY AND THE SOUL

doctrine of the Trinity this cleavage of the individual supreme deity led to an attempt to reunite the three components of the god concept at least ideationally. Yet Jesus remained the human who no longer wanted to become God, and who taught mankind to win individual spirituality through a good life.

This cleavage of the unitary god concept also produced the hero in whom the will-god as culture-hero, healer, and author returned to Earth after his heavenly task of creating the religious godhead had been completed. As an extraordinary bearer of mana the hero intervened in earthly destiny, just as medicine men and sorcerers had done at the magical stage. What had distinguished the strong-willed and successful mana bearer at the spiritual stage was the cause of his downfall during the new stage of belief in God. That is, he not only claimed all the creative power of mana for himself, but used it to set his own personal immortality against that collective, procreative immortality which was embodied in the godhead. He grasped the prerogatives already ceded to the godhead, and basked in this presumptuous likeness to God which led finally to his downfall and death. For through his deeds the hero's will made him immortal; but he lost his life for this, just as Achilles had lost his for his utterance, shameful for a Homeric hero, that he would rather be the most miserable slave on earth than king of the dead. For the soul is collective, just as immortality is procreative, and just as personal mana is no foundation for spiritual belief but only a psychology. Furthermore, as a psychology it is only one of willing and personality, and not a "normal psychology" which corresponds to collectivity. Thus the various currents within scientific psychology, and particularly the two great groups of "average" and personality psychologies, have different sources, the one arising from spiritual belief (animism), and the other from will-belief (emanism). The one is individual, resting on the idea of personal immortality; the other is collective, resting on the idea of religious immortality. The soul represents, as it were, collective willing (to be immortal), which is the will of the individual soul.

The reason why this has not been recognized and utilized psychologically before this time is twofold. First, with rare exceptions, all previous psychologies have only been interpretations of the spiritual, or forms of spiritual belief differing with each stage of consciousness and knowledge; and secondly, the psychological plane itself, in relation to which the spiritual was re-interpreted, was not understood but lay outside psychology. However, this psychological attitude which made possible the new interpretation of the spiritual was just the result of a change of willing from a positive power into a negative inhibition. That is, the psychological basis from which the new interpretation of the spiritual arose was *negative will*, which all psychology up to Nietzsche's forced into the same course that had brought the will-god over into the ethical principle of religion. Therefore the humanized will-god, the hero, finds his modern counterpart not in the psychologists, but in the poets who immortalize and perpetuate the hero in song, and in the philosophers who seek to prove the immortality of the soul metaphysically. For since will has become negative, it appears first as a problem which is manifested psychologically. Thus, all psychology and particularly its latest phase, psychoanalysis, has been an interpretation of the spiritual in the sense of negative will attitudes, and in relation to the concepts of guilt and sin. In this sense the natural science psychology which culminates in psychoanalysis is but a continuation of religious ideology and a substitute for spiritual belief, which accounts at once for its strength and its weakness.[11]

As long as will is only positive and is manifested in action, religion does not exist in any true sense, nor is psychology possible. The only possible explanation of the phenomenon of positive willing is magical and not psychological in character; it is not an "omnipotence of intellect," such as Freud finds in the inhibited willing of moralistic man, but an omnipotence of will which seems because of its incomprehensibility to stand outside the natural order and within that of the supernatural. Magic was originally a forbidden art, because it was a private one which the individual could use to his own advantage and to the detriment of others. Later it became socialized, because the sorcerer, medicine man, or priest was finally obliged to use it for the good of all. Its original significance as bad will power survived in "black" magic (as different from white or good) even as late as belief in the Devil and the black mass. Here, in the expression of positive will and in its wholesome if fateful consequences, we find the origin of moral differentiation between good and bad, which are allied in all religious systems with the ideas of light and dark. However, at the stage of positive will, it is a matter not of a moral principle but of a vital one. The arch-evils which the strong-willed mana bearer can effect are illness and death. And thus, by the incomprehen-

---

[11] In his *The Future of an Illusion* (Die Zukunft einer Illusion, 1927), Freud both approached and evaded this problem, because he wished to replace religion with science without recognizing that this goes on continuously even in psychoanalysis.

sible "effect"—natural death—evil is effected upon its denied cause which lies in the secret power of will. At this early stage of positive will expression the "cause" which was found for death lay just in man himself, even though it was ascribed to the evil of a foreign will; in the moralistic stage of religion this cause was sought and "found" in the badness and blamability of one's own will.

Originally, therefore, it was clearly a matter of projecting one's own bad will on another which led to death; but this other, evil one soon became not just any mana bearer, but a strong-willed one who otherwise eschewed tests of his will power. The bearer of collective mana, personified by the chieftain, medicine man, sorcerer, etc., became a collective evildoer who appeared in religious systems as Ahriman, Satan, or Devil. According to Persian belief, Ahriman created death, just as the Christian soul which fell to the Devil lost its immortality and really died. I believe that the change, from earthly representatives of bad collective will to the incorporation of will into a moralistic system of good and evil, is comprehensible only on the basis of a continued projection which corresponds to the denial of one's own bad willing. For the collective mana bearer did not always want to be held responsible for the unwholesome consequences of his action, and since he had relinquished a part of his mana to the spirits of the dead, he could make *them* responsible for all evil and death. But, like the chieftains whose deaths are celebrated even for a thousand days, even some of the dead were stronger in mana than were other ordinary persons such as women, whose mana was thought to be destroyed a few days after death. Both living and shadowy souls subsist on the mana which flows to them, just as the shades of the Homeric lower world were revived by drinking

strength-giving blood. Thus energetic mana led to the linguistically related *anima,* which remained just as invisible as
was the divine spouse of its Greek sister Psyche.

The will became soul because its evil effects manifested
in death were first ascribed to the living host of mana, and
then to its dead host or the soul. But just as the living mana
bearer was obliged to use his will power for good and for
healing the sick and warding off death, the immortal soul
strong in mana changed from a bad demon into a health-
bringing angel or guardian spirit. This tendency to change
illness into health and evil into good may be traced from
the earliest stage of magical will expression, through the
conflict between these two principles symbolized by religion,
to our own present moralistic, educational system. However,
this change originated in the avoidance of death, and in
the changing from a bad, death-evoking will to one that
was good, wholesome, and not destructive. Therefore, according to Christian belief, the reward for being good was
eternal life or immortality of the soul, while the punishment
for being bad was the loss of the soul. The bad will causes
death; hence, the good will may prevent it.

But originally the bad will was none other than the positive, active will; and man must first be "educated" to dedi-
cate his good willing to the service of the community. It
follows that, at the stage where the bad will was no longer
projected but was recognized as a subjective power within
the individual, will itself had to be regarded as evil, guilty,
and morally damned. However, since a psychological attitude itself was possible only at this stage of subjective
awareness of will, psychology emerged under the dominance
of moral principle, from which it is not yet free. Nietzsche
has been the only one so far to sense this problem and to

try to free both philosophy and psychology from the ban of morality. Freud's attempt to break through this vicious circle failed because he was prejudiced with a natural science ideology; he therefore recognized only the sexual manifestations of positive will power, and fell back into the morality which had been bound up inextricably with the problem since the sexual era.

We return now to our earlier explanations of the soul, in which we followed its development from an impotent shadow of the body to a fertile germ of life that included even the power of mana. If also the mana theory is now extended to reproductive processes as of the time they began to play a decisive role, it would be a mistake to identify theory and process as Freud has done in his libido theory based on sexual ideology. For the animistic world view stressed the supernatural in the concept of mana as well as in the idea of the soul. In the immortality ideology of sexuality, man found a possibility of uniting individual will and collective soul. But, from the beginning, both the individual and procreative aspects of sexuality were separated, and they have remained so in spite of all the attempts of religion, morals, and science to unite them. The sexual act was an expression of will power and life energy; reproduction symbolized a loss of mana-laden spiritual stuff, and death. Abstinence from reproduction aimed at conservation of spiritually powerful mana, just as the compulsive neurotic currently abstains from sexual intercourse in order not to die, and just as the neurasthenic fears death as a result of the sexual act. Behind moral guilt feeling is the primitive fear of death, to which Freud came much closer in his original theory of anxiety neurosis (1895) than in all his subsequent psychological explanations, which only attempted

163

to soften the impact of this fundamental insight. For the whole sexual theory of the neuroses or of anxiety was only a "therapeutic" and not a psychological theory, just as the sexual era's acceptance of procreative immortality consoled and saved man, who had lost his belief in individual immortality. Animistic man abstained from procreation in order to preserve his soul material for himself, yet affirmed his individual life strength in the sexual act as in other pleasurable acts of will. In the sexual era, reproduction was required because it served procreative immortality, but the sexual act itself was avoided because it robbed man of his strength. In a word, reproduction, which had been dangerous at first, came into favor, and sexuality, which was originally a proof of strength, became tabu.

This moralistic reëvaluation of both aspects of sex may be understood only on the basis of willing. Since will power with its unwholesome and wholesome effects corresponded to life power or mana, the negation of willing as a bad power finally led to a negation of life. The denial and projection of bad will power onto others, onto the dead, and onto God, allowed the individual a positive expression of his will; with the subjective recognition of bad will, will power as such, and that power to live which manifests itself as will, had to be denied. Thus, as an expression of will, sexuality became evil, guilty, and a cause of death; all of these characteristics had formerly been ascribed to the will. Since will could bring about death, it became labeled as bad in itself. Yet it did not simply disappear; instead it became transformed into a negative power manifested as guilt feeling, and interpreted or explained causally under the concept of sin. This was the beginning of psychology, which only deals further with the broken, denied will and with guilt as a moral phenomenon, now shorn of its former connotations of power. Parallel with this development there was the loss of naïve belief in immortality and the collective soul, which were replaced by death anxiety. Individual guilt feeling now bound the individual to the group, as belief in the collective soul had formerly done; and, like the will, sexuality became a moral instead of an energetic phenomenon, whose extreme form appears in the contemporary individual love experience. As an expression of the bad will, sexuality had to be morally justified by other individuals, since they disapproved of it and condoned reproduction only within a family structure derived from sexual ideology. The guilt that bound one to others corresponded to a psychological interpretation of the death anxiety, which appeared as a reaction to will-action branded as evil. Since will-expression necessarily led to guilt feeling, it soon became recognized that one's own bad will which had been projected on foreign or supernatural wills now threatened the life of the ego.

Just as the recognition of death invoked the animistic era, and that of procreative processes the sexual era, moralistic interpretation of one's own willing as the basis of evil produced the psychological era. For only in the last instance was it a matter of psychological knowledge in the psychological sense; in the instances of death and sexuality it was a matter of recognizing previously denied objective facts. Just as animistic theory and magical life practices represented the reaction of the current world view to the knowledge of death, the truly religious system and the moral conduct of life which corresponds to it followed recognition of the will. In both instances sexual knowledge supplied the material, or the means and content, for recasting the old ideology into a new one. This knowledge had a positive function only during the first shift from a belief in the collective soul to individual procreative immortality, because, as a consolation for a lost naïve belief in immortality, it promised continuation of life in one's own descendants. The next turning point, which resulted from denial of the ideology of procreative immortality, was characterized by the emergence of a purely religious ideology from the fusion of abandoned stages of the soul- and will-gods into a moralistic godhead symbolic of the new ego at the stage of will recognition. This evolutionary stage embodied by the Jewish deity ended with the complete collapse of antiquity in the conflict of these different ideologies, and with the beginnings of Christian ideology, which reached back to original spiritual belief and which man has long held as his last bulwark against psychological self-knowledge.

This self-knowledge, which originally concerned the will and its problems, soon turned from the ideological conflict projected onto the religious godhead, to its own consciousness and processes; and it became the object of philosophical speculation long before any psychology existed. Following a century-long detour into epistemology, Schopenhauer finally returned from the ethics of practical life conduct to the problem of willing, and thus reopened psychology's original domain. Only Schopenhauer made causal in the sense of natural science this willing in which he recognized the basic power of all living which had been characteristic of mana; and, under the pressure of moralistic ideology of negation, Schopenhauer's successor, Nietzsche, postulated will as the source of the personal power characteristic of his "superman," who represented the strong-willed mana bearer in the completely primitive sense. Although Nietzsche actually comprehended the will too specifically, he at least reaffirmed it and freed it from the moral compulsions of religion and philosophy. For both Adler who followed Nietzsche's ideology of power, and Freud who interpreted will sexually, fell back on the moral position which damned the will as bad and detrimental to the individual and society; Jung finally invoked collective morality which justified the will socially.

In my latest works, and especially in *Truth and Reality* (Wahrheit und Wirklichkeit), I tried to take the positive will as the object of psychology, and to consider it apart from its extra-psychological contents. I recognized that the deepest root of morality was not a problem of content but one of willing, and I portrayed the knowledge of evil and the guilt of willing as the fundamental bases of evil and its attendant concepts of guilt and sin. Starting from the analysis of a purely psychological problem, I arrived at a "will causality" which I contrasted with the causality concept of natural science, and which I may now round out from the spiritual standpoint. For under will causality I conceive of willing as an apparently spontaneous and incommensurable cause of visible effects, in relation to which matters of evil defy explanation, since their removal seems possible when their causes are discovered. Among these evil effects the most outstanding was death, for which various "causes" have been found or discovered from time to time. The first causality problem of man was death; but here the finding of a cause served to deny the fact.

NATURE AND SPIRIT

> *Perhaps, indeed, reality is a child which cannot survive without its nurse, illusion.*   A. S. EDDINGTON

IN 1900 THE PHYSICIST PLANCK gave the first impulse to the quantum theory, and in 1905 Einstein published his first treatise on the theory of relativity. As these theories underwent further development during the last quarter of a century, they led to the proposition "that, under the influence of the facts of atomic physics, contemporary physics earnestly doubts the practicability of a rigid causality" (Einstein).[1] Near the turn of the century, when this anti-causality movement was beginning in physics, Freud tried to apply the strict determinism of natural science to psychic events, and to demonstrate the principle of causality in mental life from which it previously had been barred.[2] About a quarter of a century later, phi-

[1] In the introduction (March 1929) to Hugo Bergmann's "The Controversy over the Law of Causality in Recent Physics" (Der Kampf um das Kausalgesetz in der jüngsten Physik) *Vieweg Sammlung*, No. 98, Braunschweig, 1929.

[2] In the *Interpretation of Dreams* (Traumdeutung) which appeared in 1900, Freud attempted to establish strict determinism in the realm of mental phenomena; and in *Three Dissertations on Sexual Theory* (Drei Abhandlungen zur Sexualtheorie), he tried to establish biology as the causal basis for psychic events.

losophers and physicists themselves began[3] to develop the epistemological implications of the new physical world view, and to regard the principle of causality as threatened by "chance" events. In ignorance of this movement, I was questioning the physical causality in Freud's determinism, and opposing "freedom of will" to such causality.[4]

Now it is well known that the subjective feeling of free will has always been the argument which philosophers have opposed to the principle of causality, and that Bergmann (p. 7) confesses that, from the time Hume raised the question until now, no one has successfully opposed this argument by bringing forth evidence to prove the validity of the law of causality. But Kant's utterly novel orientation gave the problem a new turn. Prior to precritical philosophy, science had been the image and photograph of reality. According to Kant it was rather an interpretation of reality which is governed by certain categorical premises. In Kant's sense the law of causality is a hypothesis which underlies experience. It is well known that Kant was the first to try to formulate this "antinomy" between the principle of causality which is necessary to scientific knowledge, and the principle of freedom which is indispensable to practical action.

---

[3] See the outstanding critical summary by Bergmann. In his Gifford Lectures (1927) the English professor of astronomy S. A. Eddington developed the philosophical aspects under the title, *The Nature of the Physical World*, which volume was published in 1928. (The quotation at the beginning of the present chapter comes from this book.) I knew nothing of this volume or of the literature to which it refers until I began preparing the present chapter.

[4] *Truth and Reality. An Outline of a Philosophy of Mental Life* (Wahrheit und Wirklichkeit. Entwurf einer Philosophie des Seelischen), 1929, and "The Analytic Reaction in its Constructive Aspects," in *The Technique of Psychoanalysis* (Die analytische Reaktion in ihren konstruktiven Elementen; Technik der Psychoanalyse), II, 1929. Both volumes are from the F. Deuticke Press, Vienna and Leipzig.

The value of Kant's effort lay in his formulation of the problem, which inhered in his conception of the principle of causality as a postulate imposed by man on nature, and not as a law extracted from his knowledge of nature. Hessen's work,[5] which discusses the whole problem, shows that, although Kant's attempt to solve it no longer seems acceptable, philosophy has not gone beyond this point. At least until recently, physics has behaved rather naïvely toward this conflict. It considers its own task to be "the complete emancipation of the physical account of the world from the individuality of the mind which forms it, or from anthropomorphic elements. It is the task of physics to build a world completely free from the alien elements of consciousness. This is the transcendental premise of physics" (Bergmann, p. 3). But knowledge has progressively emphasized the point that the physical world is a world of interpretation and abstraction, or, as Eddington says, a purely physical world.

> Never until now has it been so clear what a surpassing role the interpretation of facts plays in physics. Although Einstein's conception of the world has received recognizably strong support from empirical data, its greatness is in no sense to be sought in the facts themselves, but in the new meaning which it has given the empirical facts. The facts have not proved of decisive value to the world picture; it is rather the scientist's transcendental hypotheses (to use Kantian terms) which have held such a position (Bergmann, p. 1).

Here, as at other points which I shall indicate, I find myself in complete agreement with this view which marks

[5] Johannes Hessen, *The Principle of Causality* (Das Kausalprinzip), Augsburg, 1928.

170

a crisis not only in physics but in all of science. Independently of this movement in physics, and on the basis of purely psychological experiences, I sensed a crisis in psychology which approximates quite closely the collapse of the scientific world view.[5a] Only, in this connection I went a step beyond the crisis in physics, since I conceived of the psychological attitude itself which determines the meaning of facts, as an interpretation of the human microcosm based on the ideology of consciousness and will. However, I still find myself on a common footing with physics, since I did not simply hypostasize freedom of will out of subjective experience or deduce it philosophically, but was rather driven to it as the physicists had been driven to "chance," by a too strict application of determinism, to mental phenomena in this instance. I have pursued to its ultimate consequences[5b] the principle of causality which Freud applied to psychic events in a naïve "physical" way, and have been led inexorably to a point where I simply had to derive mental phenomena from a "causality of willing" in order to understand them. My conception was not that the principle of causality was "false," but that it no longer sufficed for our current level of awareness because its psychological meaning had undermined its heuristic value.

I believe that this parallel is not accidental. Man seems now to have entered a new phase of his mental evolution, which is expressed in both physics and psychology. In other

[5a] The Munich philosopher, Hugo Dingler, bases his *The Downfall of Science* (Zusammenbruch der Wissenschaft, Munich, 1926) on a failure to consider the primacy of will and its psychological sequelae.

[5b] Especially in *The Trauma of Birth* (Trauma der Geburt, 1924) where I encountered the incommensurable quantitative features of neuroses, which I discussed later in my *Genetic Psychology* (Genetischen Psychologie), Part I, 1827, 31 ff.

171

words, the modern physicist sees nature just as the modern psychologist sees man. Until recently both were ensnared in a natural science ideology whose untenability I recognized in the psychic sphere, just as certain physicists began to doubt its strict applicability to nature. On the basis of the same ideology which became so fateful for physics, Freud had fallen into the error of trying to discover behind mental phenomena a reality "free of consciousness," and of believing that he had found it in the "unconscious." He regarded his interpretations of the mental world as facts and as images of reality, just as the physicist had regarded his interpretation of the world as reality itself. But with this attempt to comprehend mental phenomena objectively, it became completely obvious that such comprehension could be mediated only by consciousness, irrespective of the subjectivity or objectivity of the observations made. To be sure, the psychological conception of this subjective influence was more difficult because the coincidence of subject and object is more marked in psychology.

In *The Trauma of Birth* (Das Trauma der Geburt, 1923), where I expanded Freud's determinism from the object (patient) to the subject (therapist), my analysis of the relation between the person "experimented upon" and the "experimenter," as this relation was manifested in the "analytic situation," weakens Freud's physical standpoint. My own orientation was a "realistic" one, which my latest work presents as a relativity psychology having no fixed standpoint for the experimenter, but only a momentarily given relationship between the experimenter and the person studied, whose closeness varies dynamically at all times. My conception primarily involved replacing a "historical" causality by an "actual" causality which, in fact, is not causality in any strict sense of the word. For according to Bergmann's formulation (p. 11): "Causality has two functions in science: (1) that of determining mutual junctures of events, and (2) that of directing the scientific treatment of sense data so that prediction of future events becomes possible." Although what I have called actual causality can satisfy the first of these demands at any given moment, the second cannot do so because its "causes" lie in a dynamic present instead of in a static past.[5c] The second requirement, namely, of achieving "prediction of future events," would be the principal task of every natural science psychology, since theory, prophylaxis, and pedagogy are based on this understanding of expected reactions. However, such reactions cannot be predicted on a basis like that which quantum theory has recently established for physics. Concerning this point, Heisenberg, who has derived the most far-reaching implications of quantum mechanics, says:[6]

[5c] Similarly, Einstein did not give up the old concept of causality, but substituted a more individual causality for it, because the theory of relativity means that every observer sees and comprehends things from his own individual standpoint, and thus has, as it were, his own "truth." However, this truth is at the same time determined spatio-temporally or dynamically; it relates to events and their intervals instead of to bodies and their distances; it concerns structure instead of material; and it has thus a greater concern for the immediate circumstances (even in explaining gravitation) than for "action at a distance" in the sense of Newtonian causality. The resultant application of the axiom of "action at point of contact," which perhaps corresponds to what I have called actual causality in the text, led to the quantum theory's recognition of "inconstancy" which shakes the principle of causality to its foundations. The relativity and quantum theories operate differently upon the principle of causality; relativity theory yields a more strict but individual causality, which ultimately means individual freedom outside the conditions of statistical, mass causality.

[6] *Zeitschrift f. Physik*, Vol. 43, 1927.—In his "The Quantum Postulate, etc." (Das Quantenpostulat, usw., in *Naturwissenschaft*, 1928), Bohr has developed a theory of complements from Heisenberg's principle of uncertainty, in consequence of which he does not exclude simultaneous perception of

> Regarding the sharp formulation of the law of causality, which asserts that if we know the present we can calculate the future, the premise and not the conclusion is false. We essentially cannot know the present in all its stages of determination . . . Because all experiments are subordinate to the laws of quantum mechanics; the invalidity of the law of causality is definitely established by quantum mechanics.

Like my relativity theory, quantum mechanics arises from a consideration of the influence of the observer, and leads to the recognition of an "inconstancy" in every sub-atomic process, which is equivalent to the admission of a certain freedom of the will in the psychic area.

As is well known, Epicurus allowed the atom (absolute chance) "the slightest deviation" from the vertical; and in his book *The Problem of Freedom of the Will* (Das Problem der Willensfreiheit, p. 153), Heinrich Gomperz arrives at a similar "spontaneity" theory according to which material elements disclose certain individual and transitory peculiarities of behavior. It appears, then, that in psychology as in physics there is greater freedom the more one advances from masses to elements, and the smaller and finer one conceives these elements to be. Psychologically, that means that the more one approaches the individual and the more completely one an-

both complements in the negligible influence of the measuring instrument. These are the causal and the spatio-temporal modes of perception as complementary and mutually exclusive characteristics of the description of the content of experience. Bohr has used this fundamental law of quantum theory, to the effect that spatio-temporal and energetic description of a process are somewhat exclusive, to account for both theories of light: the wave theory meets the needs according to the spatio-temporal concept, and the quantum theory according to the causal concept, so that there is no single theory of light, just as there is no single psychology, and for quite the same reasons.

alyzes his elements, the more difficult it becomes to justify strict determinism and causality, and the more freedom one must grant the ultimate individual elements.

> In the areas of physics concerned with the determination of temporal position, the statistical law of averages takes over just the same functions as it does in relation to prediction and reconstruction, and which the rigid law of causality previously comprehended, with the difference that under it the single case could be temporally located and reconstructed relationally in a planned way. In the sub-atomic world everything comes true only on the average. (Bergmann, p. 52.)

To this statistical law of averages, which the physicist's experience with quantum mechanics forced him to substitute for the law of causality, there corresponds in the psychological realm the "normal psychology" which derives laws of "average events" from observation, but is unable to explain the behavior of an individual in a particular situation. Hence the attempts of psychoanalysis and its various schools to achieve an individual psychology always ended in "the statistical average," as Freud's normal psychology, Adler's social psychology, and Jung's collective psychology all betray. For the individual simply lies beyond lawfulness, and cannot be fully comprehended or explained by the causality either of natural or social science. In my opinion, the only rewarding approach lies in a will psychology which includes both ways of considering the individual, yet does not attempt to understand him principally or solely on the basis of himself alone. For in the realm of psychology, too, a correct formulation of the problem seems to me more important than any attempts to solve it, which attempts may become necessary or possible only because of its faulty formulation. The error of problem formulation itself results from confusion of practical and theoretical points of view, for, with the exception of a philosophy oriented purely to spiritual matters the goal of science is not knowledge in itself, but knowledge to the end of control of nature through natural science, and of men through mental science or psychology in particular.

As I established many years ago,[7] Freud's psychoanalysis tried to synthesize this antithesis of theory and practice, but miscarried in its completely unsystematic mixture of the two points of view. His psychic causality is purely historical, in that it tries to explain the present completely in terms of the past; while, at the same time, this causal understanding is obliged to function as the therapeutically effective agent, by effecting a different manner of reacting to the present and future. However, my analysis of the "analytic situation" has shown that the therapeutic agent is simply *present experience*, and not a historical understanding in which the "therapeutic" effect seems to consist of the displacement of certain actual impulses *from* present experience. In other words, Freud's causally explained displacement into the past implies something that is practically therapeutic instead of genetically causal. That is, because we believe we can understand the present better through the past, and because we can use the past to vindicate the present, we often regard the past as causally effective when in fact it is not. This "causal" explanation may have therapeutic effects, because it serves to justify the present by implying that neurotic reactions are more infantile, for example. Regarding the theoretical aspects of

[7] *Objectives of Psychoanalysis. Relation of Theory and Practice* (Entwicklungsziele der Psychoanalyse. Zur Wechselbeziehung von Theorie und Praxis). S. Ferenczi, co-author; written in 1922, published in 1924.

this view, Adler, Jung, and others raise the objection that such a reconstruction of the past as psychoanalysis seeks through a causal understanding of the present, must remain impossible or at least unapproachable as long as one does not apply finalistic points of view.

As is well known, Aristotle differentiated at least two types of cause, efficient and final; while the quantum theory appears to make it necessary to augment causal explanation teleologically over and above a determination of the future by the past, this theory "allows and requires a determination of the past by the future" (Bergmann, p. 58). Many physicists go so far as to assume a causal effect of a sequel upon an antecedent, because certain very general laws of mechanics suggest the view that "the cause of a process depends on the end state as well as on the beginning state" (Planck). It seems, however, that even in physics we can imagine only teleologically and not causally an assumption which substitutes "the pulling power of the future for the pushing power of the past" (Riezler). Yet in this teleological sense the "pulling power of the future" in psychic events is beyond question, as the Zürich psychoanalytic school has emphasized from the beginning. But this teleological connotation of the future's influence is exactly consistent with the fortuitousness and indeterminateness of the event.

> The individual event is accidental within its limits of deviation. Precisely for this reason the event can be understood only after it has occurred. Since natural laws do not preclude chance or a state of suspension between various possibilities, the event that actually occurs can only be explained finalistically (Bergmann, p. 66, after Whitehead: *Science and the Modern World*, p. 134).

177

Although finality represents only another kind of causality, it does assume a kind of looseness in the law of causality. In physics, on the other hand, teleology introduces anthropomorphism, which Medicus formulates in his book, *Freedom of Will, and Its Limits* (Die Freiheit des Willens und ihre Grenzen, 1926, 88 ff): "Atoms seek their goal." Actually, many physicists like Eddington incline to a panpsychic world view, which has been advocated not only by Spinoza, Leibnitz, Schelling, Schopenhauer, and other Western philosophers, but by Indian philosophers as well, and which underlies the primitive's animistic conception of the world.

However, we now know that this animistic conception was founded not on a knowledge of nature or natural laws, but on the naïve projection of spiritual phenomena onto reality. And its value for our thought lies precisely in the fact that, unlike our scientific conception of the world, it could not have been derived from nature of which it was not yet aware, but that it was a projection of inner mental existence. Thus the primitive's power which animated the universe animistically was his mana, which he regarded as supernatural, obviously because he knew only its effects and not its causes. But again, just as with biological sexual processes, it is not this ignorance itself which becomes the problem for us and the primitive, but the fact that this ignorance must be maintained when it no longer really exists. This maintenance results from an act of will which I have termed *denial*. This act stands at the service of the ego which wants to conserve, preserve, defend, and justify itself. Just as it was ignorance of will process which first underlay one's need to ascribe its effects to the supernatural, it soon became a case of recognizing one's own evil-doing will, which recognition led to a self-justifying projection onto others, sorcerers, demons, gods, etc. The causes which one discovered for such processes as death and reproduction were false causes which satisfied primitive man's ostensible "hunger for a cause" because they were practical, comforting, and "therapeutic."

Although without any doubt the human mind has since found many correct causes for natural events in particular, to the extent that it was and is an interpretation of mental events, psychology still rests on the standpoint of "false" or justifying therapeutic relationships. However, by its own claim, psychoanalysis, which presumes to have discovered the "psychic reality" behind mental phenomena, is oriented therapeutically; and, in shifting responsibility from the individual, its whole causal theory is an attempt at consolation which is in no way inferior to spiritual belief or religious consolation, except that such consolation was derived from the application of the causal principle which spiritual belief had won by denial and religion had won by moralizing. As Hessen (*op. cit.*, 153) has clearly shown in accordance with philosophical knowledge of the principle of causality, "this is nothing other than an application of the logical law of causation to reality, or, more precisely, to events in the real world. However, the law of causation is only a formulation of the lawfulness of thought, and causality asserts that the structure of existence corresponds to that lawfulness. The need to think is a need to be, for thinking and being coincide. However, that means nothing more than that the world should be amenable to conceptualization." It is quite easy to bring this philosophical formulation into agreement with our psychological view, or even to translate it word for word into the language of will psychology. For what science calls "conceiving" of the world virtually means controlling the world, and, in the primitive equation of thinking and being as will-phenomena, we have recognized the identity of the need to think and the need to be. Thus the principle of causation is an intellectual form of will assertion which in its false, disciplined, causal connections is obvious, and which in its correct connections is as scientific as will causality confirms it to be.

This explains the feeling which has characterized past and present controversies about the principle of causality and, particularly, the repeated attempts to preserve this principle in spite of all experience contradictory to it, because one wants paradoxically to preserve freedom of will, of which the principle of causality is an intellectual manifestation. So perhaps it is no accident that at the moment physics began seriously to doubt the principle of causality, in the psychic area Freud's system was attempting to lend the principle the support which freedom of the will had previously withheld from it. However, since psychoanalysis had sought to compress freedom of the will into the frameworks of deterministic compulsion and causal destiny, it overstrained the causality principle by applying it to the will whose intellectual expression it was. We now find ourselves at the heart of both the causality principle as an intellectualized will principle, and of the will problem itself; for, as I explained in my will psychology, this problem is a dual one. The will, which can cause evil, can represent evil; thus the will principle becomes moral principle, and the moral principle, causal principle. In its positive expression, the will principle creates animism as a projection of itself; in its negative expression, the will creates religion as a moral justification of

180

itself; and finally, in its intellectual expression as causal principle, the will principle creates science which obtrudes nature practically and theoretically upon willing in order to justify it.

We should like to pursue further these three stages of development which stress the relation of causality to will, guilt, and consciousness respectively; yet in order not to depart too far from our theme we should keep the course of these currents in psychology before us. As recent scholars have emphatically agreed, primitive man's naïve emphasis on will left no room in his mind for causality.[8] The question of the course of unusual events was really a kind of "philosophical astonishment that anything could happen independently of willing; hence the causes that were discovered were such "will causes" as bad spirits, sorcerers, mana, or one's own mistakes, all of which could account for death. Be it a matter of naïve projection or of moral self-justification, it is always the will which is the causal factor. However, from the beginning, the setting of the problem has had a purely practical aspect which intrudes even into our scientific ideology, namely, that knowledge of causes not only makes it possible to bring about the same or different events in the future, but that such effects must be voluntary because we could not otherwise control them. The premise of magical man was the identity of thought and reality, or of willing and being; and this view underlay even those of his understandings and actions which were not causal but "fatal." That is, when anyone unwittingly carried out a voluntary act, the

[8] See especially K. Beth: *Religion and Magic* (Religion und Magie) second edition, 1927: "The Psychological Basis of Magic" (Die psychologische Grundlage der Magie), especially 168 ff.

181

fatal effect appeared not on the basis of the causal principle, but on the basis of the identity principle which rested on the will principle. "Speaking as would Levy-Brühl, there exists a feeling of mystical unity, but none of causal connection, between the rain and the rain-maker. It is a matter of introducing and activating causes, and not of producing or restoring the normal relation between the man who wants rain and rain itself" (Beth, *op. cit.*, p. 170).

As is readily seen, this fatal effect is the characteristic feature of the next stage, in which thinking and acting are no longer fatalistic but appear to be morally determined. This is the stage of religion formation at which morality rules in place of a quite different fatalistic causality.[9] This morality looks for the causes in the default of one's own will, and finds them in a justification of this will. In this sense the god of the religious stage is not only a personification of the will principle which underlies my will psychology, but also an incorporation of the causal principle as it existed under moralistic ideology. God was the cause of the world, which therefore had to be causally understandable. In other words, the strict causal principle was religious because both religion and causality represented only various expressions of the will principle at the moralistic and intellectual (scientific) stages of man's thinking. Jesus' doctrine that not a sparrow falls without God's will on earth, and Newton's discovery that no apple could fall in the absence of cosmic law, were but issues of the same will ideology. Neo-Scholasticism even used the causal principle to establish the cos-

---

[9] In Oskar Goldberg's provocative work, *The Reality of the Hebrews* (Die Wirklichkeit der Hebräer, Berlin, 1925), I find behind the causal morality of the Pentateuch (punishment for sin) the attempt to disclose the amoral succession of "error" and "catastrophe" as the basic underlying view. See especially 127 ff, "The Amoral View" (Die amoralische Auffassung).

mological proof of God.[10] The endless strife over this point between science and religion is completely meaningless because the causal principle and the will principle are basically the same.

In order to understand this identity thoroughly we must draw upon will psychology as I have developed it in my two latest works. When it is once recognized, the evil of willing necessarily leads for the most part to denial and negation of willing, and to the creation of inner as well as outer inhibitions which hinder and block expressions of will. However, these inhibitions themselves are negative will expressions, or manifestations of counter-will. Thus, in the individual as well as in the so-called compulsive neurotic, we find clear signs both of such expressions and of a conflict of will which corresponds throughout to that between godlike freedom and causal compulsion. The entire history of human development, and not merely of man's spiritual development, shows how the individual gradually negates and denies his own will in order to justify it, and how he seeks to extirpate it when justification is impossible. The law of causality is only one of many forms in which this voluntary restriction and justification of will is expressed; yet it is the characteristic form for our scientific world view, just as God was the characteristic form under the religious world view. Accordingly, the causal principle is the religion of the natural scientist by means of which he seeks to explain and govern the world, just as the adherent of religion tried to use the concept of God to these same ends.

However, at the religious stage, the scientific principle of causality corresponds not only to moral restriction of the

[10] See especially the excellent presentation by Fr. Sawicki: *The Proof of God* (Die Gottesbeweise), Paderborn, 1926.

will by God, but, to the extent that its intrusion into the spheres of will and morality miscarries, to a preservation of the will principle in the intellectual sphere. When the will is denied and replaced by sin and guilt, it experiences in the physical principle of causality an intellectual resurrection which has been threatened only recently by the physicist's intellectual, and the psychologist's epistemological, awareness. While physical theory once had to prove the divine lawfulness and meaningfulness of the world in causal terms, it now has insight into the imperfections of human conceptualization, which impels it to recognize the dominance of chance and volition. This new attitude is not a return to the omnipotence of will, but only an intellectual insight into its irrevocable loss, and it is to be characterized by what I have described as an "extirpation of God" from the world and from man. It is a process which expresses itself in the increasing influence of self-consciousness upon the consideration of facts, and whose interpretation in the sense of self-derogation has become increasingly influential. While the religious man projects his will power and his conscious moral attitude onto God, before whom he humbles himself while remaining haughty and powerful in other respects, modern man recognizes God in himself, and feels himself small and vain in comparison. He can rule nature but he cannot know it. That is, he can force his will causally, but this will itself remains as inexplicable and incalculable as natural events themselves finally are.

It is characteristic that psychology along with physics should be in the midst of a similarly humbling self-awareness. Only this "feeling of inferiority" from which we all suffer is no "neurotic complex" such as Adler intended to cure by pedagogical measures; it is much more the developmental negativism of the religious man, who no longer can have any illusions about his unimportance. We now stand at the boundary of psychology as it has grown out of spiritual belief, a psychology which leads from a projected awareness of nature to moral self-recognition and self-judgment. It does not matter whether the projection is animistic, religious, or scientific. As long as it is projection it is helpful and therapeutic, because it is illusory. With increasing self consciousness and growing self insight, this psychology becomes destructive until, with fuller awareness of the truth about one's own self, it ends in a feeling of utter powerlessness. The victory of knowledge about nature may not be crowned by one of knowledge of self, for it has to be bought with self-knowledge—too dearly. Although man's control of nature by knowledge is his greatest victory, his correspondingly greater self-awareness becomes his greatest defeat. As Nietzsche saw correctly, salvation can be expected only through a reëvaluation of guilt into will, and thus through a return to positive affirmation of will. However, this appeared impossible, so that Nietzsche's work was essentially an intellectual destruction of the old values, generated by his insight into their origins; and Nietzsche's philosophy of positive will remained incomplete and undeveloped.

Therefore psychoanalytic doctrine attacked therapeutic objectives logically enough, but ran into moral ones instead, and found itself faced with the insurmountable problem of guilt. Its "causal" explanation in terms of the Oedipus and castration complexes corresponds on the one hand to an attempt to justify will in the sense of the biological sex impulse (Oedipus), and, on the other, to judge will morally (castration) in the sense of Schopenhauer's extirpation of the "seat of will." With both of these steps, Freud has gone beyond the real psychological sphere in order to operate therapeutically, once when he justified sex, again when he judged will morally, and both times in the name of the scientific principle of causality. His causal explanation of willing, which was based on the sex impulse, was an attempt at justification; his causal explanation of will inhibition on the basis of anxiety amounted to a moralistic judgment of willing. But, in the last analysis, his whole application of the principle of causality to psychic material comprised only a disguised attempt to preserve the old will principle in the realm most proper to it. He had to fail in this attempt because the paradox of applying the causal principle to the will principle ultimately disclosed their identity. While that outcome robbed the Freudian attempt of some of its sublimity, the attempt was valuable and instructive even though the solution was typically ephemeral.

Psychoanalysis is therefore to be regarded as therapy in the most completely illusion-promoting sense of the word; for its psychology is based on the relation of the *I* to the *Thou*, whether one interprets this relation religiously as does Jung, socially as does Adler, or as infantile in the Freudian sense. It does not recognize the individual as such, but as a being whose will is "causally" explained by sexual libido, and whose consciousness is finally determined by the unconscious. Theoretically, Freud has tried to explain the entire individual causally, whereas individuality itself means extra-causality. But in therapy the will becomes of subtle importance, not only in the seemingly weak-willed neurotic, of whose performance the analyst has such a low opinion, and whose will expression the analyst interprets as "resistance"; for *the therapist's will itself* seems to be described as something almost godlike in its potency. This is not causally explained, although a situation in which one will influences another is at least conciliatory to the causal principle. Strangely enough, Freud's theory has consistently become more causal during its development. In my opinion, this happened because the theory led into a blind alley. For in the "pleasure principle," which Freud established in 1911, there still lay a certain individual "freedom," despite the apparent biological influence of the sexual character of pleasure on the principle. But the experience that man did not always behave according to the pleasure principle drove Freud to considerations which entangled him still more deeply in the causal principle instead of leading him out of it. His "Beyond the pleasure principle" could have become a "Beyond the causal principle," had he not sought shelter in a more comprehensive causality which he described as a "compulsion to repetition." However, in its significant aspects, this compulsion to repetition is controlled by the will principle; and Nietzsche, who in 1881 proclaimed "the perpetual return of the same," disclosed in *Zarathustra* that pleasure wants perpetuity and that it is the will which is responsible for the repetition compulsion. In his presentation of perpetual recurrence, Nietzsche was not completely dedicated to causality, since, in an incomparable flash of critical insight apropos of the physical concept of mechanics, he saw just the inexactness of natural law as the "necessary condition of existence and action. We would starve without it. Skepticism and foresight are always late and are seldom tolerated" (from unpublished material about the time of *Joyful Science* (Fröhlichen Wissenschaft, 1881). It appears here as elsewhere that the assimilation or direct comparison of man with the cosmos, on which mythology, religion, astrology, and science rest, only represents a wish to deny the incalculability of

187

one's own fate by an assumption of natural lawfulness. The same holds for the concept of time, of which Bergmann says,

> . . . that we fix, or as we may almost say, nominate a visible representative of absolute time sequence such as the notion of the fixed stars about the earth, which then becomes the "clock" (not for measuring time but for determining chronological order) to which we refer when deriving the time sequence, and hence the cause-effect relations, of all other events. A well-known example of this flight from uncertainty into a pseudo-objective certainty is the calendar which was originally used in Egypt, Babylon, China, Mexico, and elsewhere as a book of fate or table for evaluating particular dates as favorable or unfavorable for important undertakings.[11]

In *Truth and Reality* (Wahrheit und Wirklichkeit) I have expressed ideas concerning the psychological mechanisms, like those expressed by Nietzsche regarding the inexactness of natural law as a condition of existence. I said there (49 f) that just the false, "uncausal" connections make adaptation to reality possible, and that we are thus able to bear reality only by denying, displacing, and rationalizing it, and not by recognizing psychological truth which is destructive. As paradoxical as it may seem, the false relationships in mental or spiritual life are the real ones, for they are the causes of all the human reactions which we observe and study in psychology. However, this view implies both a dethronement of psychology as knowledge of self, and a reinstatement of ethics and epistemology in this role. For psychology can as little replace the recognition of thought, as religion and morality can be replaced. Psychoanalysis seems however to

---

[11] Th. Danzel: *Magic Man* (Der Magische Mensch), Zürich, 1928, p. 65.

raise this claim as a substitute for morality, or at least some individuals want to believe that it can be such a substitute. One would not have been able to elevate the Freudian doctrine to a new religion and morality had it not already contained such a tendency within itself. For all religion, morality, and psychology betray themselves as new and differing attempts to solve the will problem interpretatively; religion tried to solve it by projection, morality by introspection, philosophy by rationalization, and psychology by interpretation. Both religion and morality motivate causally, but fatalistically and morally, respectively; and philosophy and psychology both motivate finalistically, and rationalistically and interpretatively, respectively. However, the causal principle as such corresponds to a moralistic formulation of the will principle, and so that it cannot be applied in a psychology of the individual personality. This insight underlies the recent psychological developments of Struktur and Gestalt psychology, in which neither subject nor object is measurable or subjugated strictly to the law of causality. There are unities in place of elements; there is understanding in place of explanation, and description in place of generalization. This "modest" orientation corresponds approximately to the views of the newer physics, but like these it is too negative, too timid, or one may almost say, too intimidated. As I indicated with reference to the psychological orientation of physicists, there seems to be a tendency also for psychologists to disparage themselves. This tendency is indeed characteristic of the spirit of the times, but it tells more about the psychology of the scientists than of man.

In the present volume I have tried to conceive of psychology as a creative expression of freedom of will in the spiritual sense, since I have shown repeatedly how it grew out

189

of spiritual belief, and how it seeks to preserve the ideology of immortality, while no longer believing in the soul to which it owes its existence. First, the body itself was felt to be immortal, then the collective soul, then procreative sexuality, and finally, the individual and his collective works (science). But with man's development, the picture of the soul itself had changed. This change was reflected particularly in the bodily location of the soul, which originally was in the materials of life themselves (blood, breath), then in bodily organs important for life (liver, heart, etc.), later in the female sexual organs important for reproduction and in male sexual matter (semen), and finally in consciousness. These different localizations of the soul correspond to the animistic, sexual, and psychological eras. Thus, psychology became possible only at the fully developed stage of consciousness, in which the seat of the soul became transferred to consciousness; psychology is therefore characterized by consciousness as its inwardly oriented instrument of observation, which it focuses on the negative and already moralized phenomenon of will. Before we consider consciousness and its implications, let us glance briefly at the psychic phenomenon which consciousness itself considers and interprets at the psychological stage. At this present stage the primal, free action of positive willing appears as a *reaction* not only to outer stimuli but to inner self-established inhibitions and resistances which are just as "causal" as external stimuli. Freedom of the will appears only as a denial of compulsion, and what remains of free, positive willing becomes rationalized morally as compulsive causation, fatal necessity, or justification. Thus the psychic phenomena with which psychology deals are absolute opposites of the primal, mental, or spiritual

190

events in which guilt-free projection of positive free will predominated.

As the seat of the soul, consciousness, which stands opposed to these phenomena at the psychological stage, has another meaning besides that of reflecting natural events. It had mediated man's knowledge, if not his recognition, of sexual processes and death; and yet, at the same time, it had become a kind of insurance against death. It did this in two ways: first, in the dream, which provided a more continuous awareness of existence of a self permanently threatened by life; and secondly, in a higher, broader sense, in which it proves its existence by representing the seat of the soul. Thus there appears finally the paradox that man feels immortal just because of his fleeting consciousness, which death extinguishes; and that he remains convinced of the frailty and transitoriness of his body, which primitive man believed existed forever. Death, which was recognized by consciousness, was denied by individual self-consciousness; and this self-consciousness interpreted the psychic phenomenon of will in its own sense. No wonder then that psychology, and particularly psychoanalysis, which never analyzed the observing consciousness itself, has yielded only self-deception, just like the original spiritual belief from which it descended, and which, in spite of its own testimony to the contrary, it still tries to preserve.

Here lies the cardinal error from which natural science suffers. The soul may not exist, and, like belief in immortality, it may prove to be man's greatest illusion; nevertheless it must picture not only the objects, but the content, of psychology, whose objects are not things or facts but ideas and ideologies. And, like our entire human reality, which includes

191

scientific psychology, these same ideologies are products of spiritual belief. Psychology has to do only with interpretations of spiritual phenomena in and of themselves, and as they refer to the individual self, whether they are already objectified or are still subjective. However, interpretation itself is nothing but an intellectualized will phenomenon, and while it may therefore be a matter of interpretation of the external world, of other humans, or of one's own self, there always lies in this kind of understanding an actual "handling" in the real sense of the word, a taking possession of a thing, a violation, a creation in the sense of one's own ego and in the likeness of one's self. The creative person fashions the world according to his conscious, willing ego; the neurotic type interprets it psychologically according to his moralistic, guilt ego; and the psychotic identifies himself with it in the sense of his magic, spiritual ego.

Just as animism was the ideology of the primitive era, as sexual ideology was characteristic of antiquity, and as the Middle Ages comprised the era of Christian ideology, so psychological ideology rules today. This is meaningful only in relation to our explanations, and particularly to the one depicting contemporary psychology not only as a science for the explanation of mental and other phenomena but as a continuation of, and a substitute for, this spiritual phenomenon which fashions the contemporary ideology that governs our conception and alteration of our world. However, psychology, which is gradually trying to supplant religious and moral ideology, is only partially qualified to do this, because it is a preponderantly negative and disintegrating ideology, and an ideology of resentment in Nietzsche's sense. It destroys illusions and ideologies, which can no longer withstand its progressive self-consciousness. It becomes progressively unable to maintain even itself, and finally, as the last natural science ideology, it destroys itself. Therefore psychology cannot replace morality, because all attempts to set natural law in place of the rules created by human willing have generally not proved feasible in physics, biology, or psychology. For, as Kant first recognized, so-called natural laws are only outward projections of the laws of individual willing; and the famous parallel between the "starry heavens above me" and the "moral law within me" properly exists not because morality corresponds to a lawfulness of the cosmos, but because the cosmos is interpreted morally in the sense of a higher, divine will.

The insecurity of the causality principle of natural science can be traced in biology as in physics. Only, its influence on the collapse of psychological ideology is more evident, particularly because psychoanalysis has overstressed the biological factor in favor of the moral one. For man lives basically not as a biological organism alone but as a moral being as well, and this bipolarity accounts for all his problems. In the biological sphere his will manifests itself as action, and in the moral sphere as reaction. The task of all education and therapy is to reconvert this reaction into action, or to translate compulsion of will into freedom of will. But in the biological sphere there already rules a "freedom" like that in physics, which pertains to the inorganic "cell" or atom. For biology reduced to chemistry cannot reconstruct organic cellular life "causally," and, according to the most incisive explanations by Weismann, death seems to be only "accidental" and not "necessary."[12] He proposes that "in the single-celled

---

[12] August Weismann: *Concerning Life and Death. A Biological Study* (Ueber Leben und Tod. Eine biologische Untersuchung), second edition, Jena, 1892.

organism there is essentially no 'natural death,' or death from inner causes" (*op. cit.*, p. 17). Only with the multicellular organism, which reproduces by "propagation" rather than by division, is there a natural death. And in this instance, death pertains only to the somatic and not to the reproductive cells. Thus modern biology not only recognizes a kind of immortality, but, like primitive belief, it also finds that "the most intimate cause of death is actually reproduction" ("the further and deeper, however, that life power is standardized relative to the duration and output of the period of reproduction") (*op. cit.*, p. 65).

In one of the foregoing paragraphs I called psychology the last natural science ideology, because of all interpretation it is the one that concerns the interpretative instrument itself, which is the spiritual and feeling life of man. But it is not clear why the interpretation of just *this* bit of nature by human consciousness should yield truths of greater certainty or longer life than should the interpretation of other phenomena by a self-consciousness which is individually and temporally conditioned and utterly changeable. Even in psychology, and perhaps there more than elsewhere, it seems to be just a matter of proclaiming a new, current interpretation, yet not *as* an interpretation or even as the reality which underlies any interpretation. The only reality which exists in the psychic realm is the Now: the same Now which the physicist finds so incomprehensible, inapplicable, or simply inconceivable. Herein lies one of the most fundamental distinctions between natural science psychology and its methodological prototype, physics. For, as already noted, it is the "task of physics to construct a world of objects from which consciousness is completely excluded" (Bergmann, *loc. cit.*, p. 25); while psychology, by way of complete contrast, is concerned with a world built exclusively of consciousness. In his Academy treatise, "Causal Structure of the World and the Difference between Past and Future" (Kausalstruktur der Welt und der Unterschied von Vergangenheit und Zukunft), the physicist Reichenbach has tried to use a topological formulation of causality relationships to establish the Now-point as the border between past and future without going back to physical factors. Bergmann quite properly questions Reichenbach's success, since "the concept of the Now is bound up intimately with that of the ego" (*op. cit.*, p. 28). Freud wanted in a completely physical sense to explain psychic phenomena causally in relation to the past, and so to mediate the predetermination of such phenomena in the sense of prophylaxy and therapy. But in doing this he neglected the real psychic object, *the currently operating ego and its Now,* which even physics finally found imponderable and which psychology cannot treat because it concerns only actual, current, conscious phenomena.

For if I may so put it, psychology has still less to do with facts than has physics. It cannot in the least exclude consciousness, and since it cannot do this, it is not a natural science in the sense of physics or biology at all, but a science of relationships and relativities. Thus psychology is at no time an interpretation of facts such as one finds in physics and biology, but an interpretation of the attitudes of the individual self, which we project on others through the medium of so-called objective psychology. Psychology is interpretation of self in others, just as physics is interpretation of self in nature. In this sense, psychology is self-affirmation or self-assertion, and psychology as self-knowledge is self-deception or belief, for man's psychological creed is immortality.